"John Hawthorne is a seasoned veteran of Christian higher education, and his thoughtful and provocative reflections will be sure to spark important conversations among college and university leaders as they seek to navigate a challenging and uncertain future."

—**Rick Ostrander**
Michigan Christian Study Center

"Drawing on his expertise as a social scientist and decades of experience in Christian higher education, Hawthorne diagnoses the cultural, institutional, and demographic challenges facing Christian colleges and universities—especially those led by fear of change and perceived threats from the outside world. Hawthorne offers an alternative vision of the Christian university in which faculty, students, and administrators cooperate in crafting and living out their core values with courage and hope for the future. This book is a valuable resource to those concerned about the present state of Christian higher education and anyone interested in a fresh paradigm that places liberal learning at the center of the Christian university."

—**Scott M. Coley**
author of *Ministers of Propaganda*

"Whether I agree or disagree with him, no one makes me think more deeply, critically, and creatively about Christian higher education than John Hawthorne. Drawing on his extensive experience as a professor, administrator, and accreditation peer reviewer, John offers knowledgeable analysis of the challenges facing Christian universities and a hopeful vision for their future. Thought-provoking and wide-ranging, *The Fearless Christian University* will be especially valuable reading for the leaders whose decisions now will shape their institutions for years to come."

—**Christopher Gehrz**
Bethel University

THE FEARLESS
CHRISTIAN UNIVERSITY

—

John W. Hawthorne

WILLIAM B. EERDMANS PUBLISHING COMPANY
GRAND RAPIDS, MICHIGAN

Wm. B. Eerdmans Publishing Co.
2006 44th Street SE, Grand Rapids, MI 49508
www.eerdmans.com

Book design by Lydia Hall

Printed in the United States of America

31 30 29 28 27 26 25   1 2 3 4 5 6 7

ISBN 978-0-8028-8456-5

Library of Congress Cataloging-in-Publication Data

A catalog record for this book is available from the Library of Congress.

To my most faithful conversation partner, Jeralynne,
who not only introduced me to people in Christian higher education
and followed me across the country
but has been an active and sometimes passive participant
in many of the conversations that birthed this book

Contents

Preface

I couldn't have written this book if I was still employed by a Christian university. I'm not saying that someone would have stopped me. However, it would have provided an opportunity for one of those "We just want to make sure you're still on board with our mission" conversations. I had enough of those conversations without having to deal with what's in this book.

Much of what you will read has been percolating for over forty years. Late in my graduate school coursework I had significant angst about my professional direction. On the one hand, I had role models who were committed Christians working on the sociology of religion at state schools, which seemed an attractive path. On the other, I saw that Christian colleges in the early 1980s could deepen their commitments to academic excellence, especially in the field of sociology. Amid my professional struggles, a professor at my wife's alma mater, Olivet Nazarene College (now University), resigned. I was asked to take the position. So, the decision was made for me.

Early in my time at that institution, I partnered with a colleague to explore precisely what made a Christian university Christian. Was it the faculty, the curriculum, the community, the denomination? How did theological commitments translate into academic objectives? We wrote conference papers and had lots of conversations, but it didn't really go anywhere. This book is the culmination of a project I started four decades ago.

During my time at Olivet Nazarene, I was increasingly involved in various aspects of university life and close to senior administrators. I served on the university curriculum committee and the student life council. It led me to conclude that perhaps administration was something I wanted to do (even though many faculty run from the thought).[1]

When I left Olivet Nazarene for Sterling College (in Kansas), it was partly to pursue a role in administration. It was a smaller school in terms of enrollment and faculty, but that made it easier to have conversations about core identity. As the college took over a nontraditional degree program for working adults (in Missouri) after another school closed, I eventually became vice president of that program. Curiously, that experience made me consider more deeply the needs of traditional students. When I was recommended to take the chief academic officer role at Warner Pacific College (now University) in Portland, Oregon, I jumped at the chance.

Warner also was small and had a history of financial struggles. It had experienced accreditation challenges, having just survived a show-cause order. Three things stand out from my time at Warner. First, I got to work closely with the responsible accrediting body (work that I enjoy all these years later). Second, I got to build up the faculty both in terms of relieving their fear of closure and in terms of vibrant hires. Third, I developed an interest in the ethos of academic institutions—particularly, the ways in which a university's history both defined its present and limited its imagination.

From Warner I went to serve as provost at Point Loma Nazarene University in San Diego. It was significantly larger, with a highly developed institutional culture that leaned toward the status quo. It is also one of the most beautiful campuses in America, overlooking the Pacific Ocean. During my time there, I tried to work with faculty to explore Point Loma's Wesleyan identity and to revise the general ed-

1. Daniel W. Drezner, "You Could Not Pay Me Enough to Be a College President," *Chronicle of Higher Education*, December 14, 2023, https://tinyurl.com/5y899d6c.

ucation program around holistic education. It was there that I noticed the ways that students were changing from what I had known early in my career. While there were specific conflicts within the institution, it was the gap between my educational philosophy and that of other administrators that eventually led to me losing that position.

I ended my career on the faculty of Spring Arbor University in Michigan. I taught sociology, criminal justice, and general education courses. I served as sociology department chair, social science division chair, chair of the faculty, and accreditation liaison officer. Thanks to an internal grant, I wrote my previous book introducing freshmen to the Christian university environment.[2] I retired from Spring Arbor in May 2020 and moved to the Denver area in 2021 to be near family.

While the initial seeds of this book can be traced to those early conversations at Olivet Nazarene, experiences in all my institutions and roles have nurtured those seeds. I was privileged to see students become university leaders themselves. I worked with administrators who weren't academics. I learned about the concerns of trustees and of their tendency toward conflict avoidance. I had faculty colleagues who could provide a robust defense of liberal arts institutions and others who really didn't see the point. I saw that far too many conversations ended over concern about "what church people would think."

This book, then, is an exercise in reimagining. What if Christian universities embraced their identity as academic institutions, with all the riskiness that implies? What could those institutions accomplish if they weren't so afraid?

The layout of the book is as follows. Chapter 1 addresses the problem of fear and the ways it unnecessarily limits Christian university thinking. Chapter 2 explores the question of university mission and suggests ways that the mission of Christian universities needs to be rethought considering today's students. Chapter 3 challenges the notion of teaching a Christian worldview and outlines the kind of academic ethos that will benefit students long after they graduate.

2. John W. Hawthorne, *A First Step into a Much Larger World: The Christian University and Beyond* (Eugene, OR: Wipf and Stock, 2014).

Chapter 4 tackles the tendency of Christian universities to get caught up in the culture war and suggests ways of easing those tensions. Chapter 5 examines relationships between administrators, trustees, and faculty and offers ways to eliminate tension and improve institutional alignment.

Chapter 6 addresses the challenge of enrollment given the impending "demographic cliff" and the decreasing percentage of students who identify as evangelical. Chapter 7 calls for administrators and trustees to truly engage the needs of students as they are, not as we might wish they were. Chapter 8 attempts to reframe the relationship between the Christian university and the church by considering the university as a mission outpost rather than an extension of the church. Chapter 9 concludes the book by providing a fictionalized account of one fearless Christian university and another institution on the way.

To my readers: Be fearless! Now more than ever, the world needs Christian higher education to be bold in addressing the needs of contemporary society.

The Limits of Fear

Christian universities,[1] much like the evangelical subculture that spawned them, are characterized by fear: fear of societal decline, fear of secular authorities, fear of apostasy, fear of not being "real" schools. In short, they fear losing their way.

Scholars have long identified the ways that this fear is expressed within the broader evangelical world. Historians John Fea and Kristin Kobes Du Mez document the ways in which an oppositional view toward those on "the outside" has led to contemporary stances of separatism.[2] Sociologists Christian Smith and James Davison Hunter argue that the opposition to the broader secular world is essential to

---

1. Throughout this book, I use the term *Christian university* to describe those schools that are expressions of the evangelical subculture. It is true that some of them retain *college* in the name, but *Christian colleges and universities* is cumbersome. It is also true that some Catholic schools may share many characteristics described herein, as do some institutions affiliated with the Church of Jesus Christ of Latter-Day Saints. Finally, while Bible colleges and ministerial institutes have significant overlap with Christian universities, they are different enough to be outside the scope of this book.

2. John Fea, *Believe Me: The Evangelical Road to Donald Trump* (Grand Rapids: Eerdmans, 2018). Kristin Kobes Du Mez, *Jesus and John Wayne: How White Evangelicalism Corrupted a Faith and Fractured a Nation* (New York: Liveright Publishing, 2020).

evangelical identity.[3] It is as if there is always a concern that "they" will disrupt how "we" are trying to live.

Molly Worthen explains this concern in *Apostles of Reason*, arguing that evangelicals face "three elemental concerns that unite them: how to repair the fracture between spiritual and rational knowledge; how to assure salvation and a true relationship with God; and how to resolve the tension between the demands of personal belief and the constraints of a secularized public square."[4] It is easy to see how these "three elemental concerns" become problematic for Christian universities. As Adam Laats observes in *Fundamentalist U*, defining the boundaries between acceptable educational exploration and "going secular" has been a challenge for Christian universities since their earliest days.[5]

Concerns might arise from conservative critics at any point. Sociologically, boundaries are defined only by violation. Because various stakeholders lack a clear understanding of exactly how a Christian university is supposed to operate, demarcations of what is acceptable are fuzzy at best. University leaders operate far too often out of concern that a boundary will inadvertently be crossed and, as a result, that their institution's reputation will be damaged, donations will dry up, and the school will be characterized as "going liberal."[6]

---

3. Christian Smith, *American Evangelicalism: Embattled and Thriving* (Chicago: University of Chicago Press, 1998); James Davison Hunter, *American Evangelicalism: Conservative Religion and the Quandary of Modernity* (New Brunswick, NJ: Rutgers University Press, 1983); James Davison Hunter, *Culture Wars: The Struggle to Define America* (New York: Basic Books, 1991); James Davison Hunter, *To Change the World: The Irony, Tragedy, and Possibility of Christianity in the Late Modern World* (New York: Oxford University Press, 2010).

4. Molly Worthen, *Apostles of Reason: The Crisis of Authority in American Evangelicalism* (New York: Oxford University Press, 2014), 4.

5. Adam Laats, *Fundamentalist U: Keeping the Faith in American Higher Education* (New York: Oxford University Press, 2018).

6. A new membership group of Christian universities launched in January 2020. While the International Alliance for Christian Education says it is in

There is another way forward for Christian universities. Christian higher education has a unique value that depends upon neither separation from the broader culture nor fear of departing from the narrow path.

I am advocating for a *fearless Christian university*: an institution that understands its role in the higher education landscape, can articulate that position in meaningful ways, organize its people and programs in support of that mission, and become a laboratory for how people of faith engage the broader culture. There are numerous forces that mitigate against my vision, and many of the shifts that have occurred in Christian universities (more below) may well have to be addressed if the fearless Christian university is to be seriously pursued.

CHRISTIAN UNIVERSITIES AND RECENT CHANGES

Numerous forces internal to Christian higher education, when combined with broader societal changes in recent decades, require us to rethink the idea of a Christian university. The convergence of various factors makes the former oppositional stance no longer tenable.

I'll begin with the internal changes. Recent decades have seen a change in faculty identity, from being ministry focused to being discipline focused. While younger faculty still attempt to authentically engage their Christian students, they do so as disciplinary experts. In the early part of my career, schools bragged about the growing percentage of faculty with doctorates. This practice disappeared as having a doctorate in hand (or close to it) became de rigueur for hiring.

---

partnership with larger groups like the Council for Christian Colleges and Universities (CCCU), its membership comes from the more conservative side of the Christian university movement. According to its "Mission and Vision" statement, it claims to promote "collective conviction around biblical orthodoxy and orthopraxy, [and] cultural witness," https://iace.education/mission. Two former presidents of the CCCU are on its board of reference. It's not a stretch to imagine that a separation with the CCCU might occur if the latter is seen as too culturally accommodating.

Even those hired at a master's level were encouraged to complete a doctorate as soon as possible. Faculty going through doctoral programs devote themselves to understanding a unique segment of their discipline. The expectation that they will continue their scholarship is ingrained in them, even though scholarship may not be particularly celebrated at their institutions.

In the last few decades, administrators have become more disconnected from faculty. Today, faculty are often in the dark about issues of institutional direction, and the administration tends to view faculty as obstacles to progress who don't see the real threats the university is under. And some administrators have grown distrustful of faculty. When faculty members begin asking questions about an administrative decision, no matter how benign, it is seen as a mark of disloyalty. One of the presidents I served under, speaking at an opening-of-school dinner, said, "Those who rock the boat will find themselves on the rocks."

To be fair to the administrators, managing even a healthy Christian university became far more challenging over this period. The demographic realities that were forecast in the 1980s came to pass. There were fewer high school graduates, and an increasing percentage of those were people of color. College costs, even with tuition discounting, moved out of reach for many families, who developed an aversion to debt of any form. Competition from state schools and community colleges intensified. The financial crisis of 2007 to 2009 affected schools and families alike, accelerating existing trends.

One way of mitigating these trends was to expand programming in new avenues beyond the traditional student population. For many Christian universities, a door opened through programming for working adults. Courses could be offered in the evenings, one or two nights a week, allowing adult students who had been out of the higher education marketplace for years to try to earn a credential.[7] Graduate

---

7. Prior to the rise of for-profit behemoths, these programs were lifesavers for smaller Christian universities. Over time, many of these nontraditional programs foundered in the face of competition and the difficulty of maintaining new markets.

programs followed, first in education and then in business. Online programming followed later.[8]

This diversification of program types provided a significant buffer against the decline in the number of traditional students. It also exponentially increased the complexity of the data that administrators were trying to manage. Numerous variables affected each modality, and it wasn't uncommon for multiple program offerings to struggle simultaneously.

This put many small and mid-sized institutions into continual crisis mode. Each fall would bring an explanation of which variables had behaved in surprising ways, creating the fiscal crisis for the current year (which looked a lot like last year's fiscal crisis). More cost cutting and striving for efficiency resulted. Vacancies were left unfilled, programs shrunk, and attempts to gain new markets (new STEM programs, additional athletic teams) were funded as the latest solution.

Denominational identity declined over the same period.[9] Whereas denominational schools may have been dominated by students from the founding denomination in the 1980s, increasingly students came to the Christian university from a variety of denominational traditions (or from no religious tradition at all). Students in the new modalities didn't experience the Christian campus environment essential to the residential program. Many students in these programs felt more affinity with their cohort or their location than with the university. The mission of the institution often became generically Christian, dependent upon stock phrases featured on its letterhead and orientation materials.

This trend toward generic Christianity presents an interesting paradox. During my experience at five institutions, I became highly aware of the ways in which the university's dominant ethos was shaped by its denominational and institutional history. Yet the faculty and students who were part of its core mission, while affirming Christian educational values, were disconnected from that rich history and ethos. Re-

---

8. I look at these programs in more detail in chapter 6.

9. Ryan Burge, "How Many Evangelicals Are There?," Substack, December 28, 2023, https://tinyurl.com/yc8e7pze.

gardless of how compelling the institution's mission statement might be, how it would shape institutional practice was left to a variety of interpretations.

The traditional student population has changed over the last four plus decades as well. When I started teaching, it was not surprising to hear Christian university administrators bragging that the unrest of the sixties (roughly 1965 to 1974) had bypassed their campuses. Students focused on their classes, social activities, and relationships and were somewhat remote from the outside world.

This wasn't true for all students. Some were passionate about injustice and poverty (especially overseas). Over time, the size of this group grew, and their concerns began to become sharper.

This shift in orientation became clearer to me late in the first decade of the twenty-first century. Student government leaders at my university requested that the administration approve a forum on LGBTQ+ issues. While the administration wanted to create a task force—made up primarily of cabinet members and trusted others— to explore the issue from a scriptural foundation, the students wanted to talk openly about how Christians could embrace the complexity of the larger LGBTQ+ question.

This trend accelerated and permeated student bodies over the next decade. Even prior to *Obergefell*, students had gone to school with friends who had come out long ago. It wasn't an abstract question for them but a recognition of the identity of their friend. I'll often return to institutional concerns about LGBTQ+ accommodation, because it's a tension point that both illustrates why a fear-based, oppositional stance is limited and presents a path forward for more fearless institutions.

The same patterns are evident with race. As much as Christian universities make claims about commitments to diversity, equality, and inclusion, students expect action. They are increasingly impatient with lackluster responses to racial injustice. A meme goes viral on campus, and students expect quick and decisive reaction from the administration. Black Lives Matter, police shootings, and structural inequality are concerns for many students. Given their facility with social media, communication and organizing are far easier than they were even two decades ago.

A 2023 update from the Barna Group demonstrated that significant numbers of the rising generation (persons aged thirteen to seventeen) place high importance on these issues.[10] Over a third of their sample placed a high priority on resolving economic inequality, fighting sexual abuse, dealing with hunger, or promoting better mental health. Nearly as many identified resolving racial injustice as important. Such numbers suggest that these issues are not optional for Christian universities but matters they will be expected to engage.

WHY THE STATUS QUO ISN'T ENOUGH

Christian universities are generally unprepared for the changes I've outlined. Donors, trustees, denominational leaders, and cultural gatekeepers tend to be older and more conservative than the faculty and students. Conflict is almost inevitable. Where in the early part of my career donors were concerned about the students holding air guitar concerts or dances on campus, today's students are asking for LGBTQ+ support groups.[11]

Most of these older conservative leaders have little background in higher education beyond their experience as a student. Faculty commitments and priorities seem foreign to them. They ignore faculty members until something is perceived as a crisis. Because the admin-

---

10. Barna Group, "Five Causes Today's Teens Care About," *Barna Highlight*, March 13, 2023, https://tinyurl.com/34ya82sc.

11. Jonathan S. Coley, *Gay on God's Campus: Mobilizing for LGBT Equality at Christian Colleges and Universities* (Chapel Hill: University of North Carolina Press, 2018); Jonathan S. Coley, "Reframing, Reconciling, and Individualizing: How LGBTQ Activist Groups Shape Approaches to Religion and Sexuality," *Sociology of Religion* 81, no. 1 (Spring 2020): 45–67.

istration is generally conflict averse (and the president's job depends upon staying in the good graces of those leaders), troublesome faculty members are often deemed expendable.

While these internal changes were happening, external perceptions of Christian universities shifted significantly too. One of my institutions frequently referred to itself as "the best-kept secret" in the region. It was doing great work in affecting its graduates, the claim went, but the broader society never seemed to notice. But this could be said of nearly all Christian universities, as the mainstream media tend to focus on elite private or flagship universities. Nevertheless, it doesn't take much for a Christian university to break into the news cycle, and usually not in a good way.

Readers might occasionally run across a story about Christian universities in the *Chronicle of Higher Education*, *Inside Higher Ed*, or *Christianity Today* but not in the mainstream media.[12] Although institutions may send out rafts of press releases, the vast majority are ignored.

But the advent of social media, the tool of choice in a burgeoning call-out culture, changed all that. In recent years, Christian universities have been increasingly present in the media ecosystem. Christian universities can no longer assume that they work in secret. A chapel speaker goes off the rails, a president makes an unfortunate statement to a group of students or donors, an athletic team engages in misogynistic acts, and it doesn't take long for evidence and commentary to show up on TikTok, Snapchat, Instagram, Threads, X, or Facebook feeds. Alumni organize in response, and the media run stories on alumni discontent.

In 2021, the podcast *Gangster Capitalism* ran a nine-part series on Jerry Falwell Jr. and problems at Liberty University.[13] It came on the heels of a very public break between the former president and the

12. Liam Adams, "Christian Colleges Are Changing to Survive. Is it Working?," *Christianity Today*, September 9, 2020, https://tinyurl.com/2ncum9pm.

13. "Season 3: Jerry Falwell Jr. and Liberty University," in *Gangster Capitalism*, podcast, produced by Andrew Jenks, Audacity Studios, 2021, https://tinyurl.com/2p9jj4ee.

university. The series did a deep dive into the organizational culture of Liberty. While Liberty may be an outlier in a review of Christian institutions, the idea of protecting the brand at all costs runs throughout many universities.[14] But once the media attention starts, protecting the brand becomes very difficult. In 2022, the troubles of Jerry and Becki Falwell and how they related to Liberty University became a salacious documentary shown on Hulu for all the world to see.[15]

Another external factor affecting Christian universities is the changing religious landscape in America, especially among the youngest generation. According to the 2022 Census of American Religion conducted by the Public Religion Research Institute (PRRI), only 9 percent of respondents aged eighteen to twenty-nine identified as white evangelical Protestants.[16] In contrast, over a third identified as unaffiliated.

This rise of the nones has four noteworthy consequences for Christian universities. First, because white evangelicals have historically been the primary market for Christian universities, with that population shrinking by 10 percent over the past forty years, the base market for Christian institutions is much smaller and competition for that segment more fierce. Second, that increased competition tends to push schools to try to become more conservative to capture market share. Third, and paradoxically, the need to hold on to market share likewise encourages schools to accept the more progressive student voices described above.[17] Fourth, a decline in religious affiliation means that a greater share of the general public is more

---

14. A similar pattern can be seen in the Southern Baptist Convention's struggles over how to deal with (or avoid) long-running concerns about sexual abuse by pastors. See Robert Downen, Lise Olsen, and John Tedesco, "Abuse of Faith," *Houston Chronicle*, February 10, 2019, https://tinyurl.com/y2fd6ffh, and *Christianity Today*'s podcast series *The Rise and Fall of Mars Hill*, 2021, https://tinyurl.com/bdck6udp.

15. *God Forbid: The Sex Scandal That Brought Down a Dynasty*, directed by Billy Corben, 2022.

16. Public Religion Research Institute, *The 2022 Census of American Religion*, February 24, 2023, https://tinyurl.com/y2x98bkh.

17. More on this in chapter 6.

likely to see Christian universities as an anachronistic reflection of an earlier era.

Many Christian universities see themselves as holding the line against secular incursion. This self-perception is consistent with PRRI data appearing right before the 2020 election.[18] As part of that survey, researchers found that 66 percent of white evangelicals believe that Christians face a lot of discrimination, the largest area of agreement across several subgroups measured. By contrast, only 37 percent of all Americans and 20 percent of the unaffiliated agreed.

The more, then, that Christian universities see themselves as oppressed by the broader society, the less will their position be understood by many Americans. This disconnect will, in turn, make them seem out of touch with society as a whole and likely to face scrutiny and disapproval from the culture at large.[19] This pattern of alienation has been exacerbated in recent years, as evangelicals have increasingly been seen as supporting Republicans, especially former president Donald Trump. The more political these institutions are assumed to be, the less likely they are to be given the benefit of the doubt.[20]

A final external factor to consider is one endemic to all of higher education: the general trend toward questioning whether college is worth it. Driven in part by concern over high levels of loan debt held by graduates, a cottage industry of pundits has been lauding the value of trade professions, bemoaning specialized majors at expensive institutions, and pontificating about the high cost of tuition.[21]

18. Public Religion Research Institute, *Dueling Realities: Amid Multiple Crises, Trump and Biden Supporters See Different Priorities and Futures for the Nation*, October 19, 2020, https://tinyurl.com/mr47jt38.

19. This is the topic of chapter 4.

20. Lydia Bean, *The Politics of Evangelical Identity: Local Churches and Partisan Divides in the United States and Canada* (Princeton, NJ: Princeton University Press, 2014); Michele F. Margolis, *From Politics to the Pews* (Chicago: University of Chicago Press, 2018).

21. These pundits often fail to recognize (1) that much of the explosion of student debt came from graduate, professional, and for-profit programs and less from traditional programs, (2) that the return on investment for a

These public sentiments about the value of education have affected Christian universities. Many students are choosing between a Christian college and a local state school or community college. They are being asked to invest scarce financial resources for the marginal value of a Christian community with classes taught by Christian faculty. The situation has been made worse by an increased focus on niche, job-related programs at the expense of the traditional liberal arts that characterize most Christian universities. For many, the liberal arts are a questionable choice. If one is looking for the biggest short-term bang for the buck, the Christian university may look too much like a luxury purchase.

THE SHAPE OF FEAR

Christian universities have long argued that they are distinct from secular schools. One may argue that the difference between Christian universities and their secular counterparts can be easily identified: Bible and theology requirements, campus lifestyle agreements barring certain behaviors, and chapel services multiple times per week. Or perhaps the difference lies in what the Council for Christian Colleges and Universities (CCCU) refers to as "the integration of faith and learning." This latter approach assumes that there are uniquely Christian ways of teaching sociology or biology or English or management. As part of supporting a "Christian worldview," a faculty member might highlight those elements of the discipline that are most consonant with the faith and downplay other elements.[22]

I submit that the heart of the distinction between Christian universities and secular schools is the fear of students losing their way. Perhaps they would be tempted by the (often imaginary) licentious

---

four-year degree is still nearly a million dollars in lifetime earnings, (3) that most students don't attend Ivy League institutions or major in art history, and (4) that gross tuition is not the same as net tuition.

22. More on this in chapter 3.

lifestyle of secular schools, so we need campus lifestyle covenants. Perhaps they would drift away from faith once they have separated from family and their home church, so we need chapel services. Most importantly, they might be led astray by faculty members who attack Christianity, so we need careful hiring practices.[23]

A fear-based, oppositional stance characterizes too much of the Christian university sphere. A recent example of this fear may be seen in conservative Grove City College's reaction to an alumni petition, feeling the need to communicate to the world that it had not "gone woke."

> Jemar Tisby, author of *The Color of Compromise*, spoke about his book in a Grove City College chapel in October 2020.[24] A year later, some alumni and parents submitted a petition decrying Tisby's chapel address, the existence of a diversity initiative, and courses that assigned books on combating racism. Consider this from the petition: We are concerned. From what we've observed, a destructive and profoundly unbiblical worldview seems to be asserting itself at GCC, threatening the academic and spiritual foundations that make the school distinctly Christian. That worldview is Critical Race Theory (CRT).[25]

The petition was major news in evangelical spaces, and the trustees responded by appointing a special committee to conduct an institutional review to demonstrate the stability of Grove City's conservative

---

23. This is not just rhetoric from the latest *God's Not Dead* movie. I had a campus chaplain in the early 1990s tell me that the purpose of chapel was to correct what faculty like me were doing the rest of the week.

24. Jemar Tisby, *The Color of Compromise: The Truth about the American Church's Complicity in Racism* (Grand Rapids: Zondervan, 2019); Jemar Tisby, "An Open Letter to the Board of Trustees at Grove City College," Substack, May 18, 2022, https://tinyurl.com/u8n82cte.

25. "Save GCC from CRT," updated November 10, 2021, https://tinyurl.com/3xhcb96y.

credentials. In their report, the committee writes, "CRT is incompatible with GCC's vision, mission, and values for many reasons" and goes on to attribute, with no supporting evidence, various malicious attitudes and actions to CRT as such.[26] After making several recommendations to assuage the critics, the committee concludes: "To the petitioners and outside observers who may have wondered if Grove City College is going 'woke,' the answer is emphatically no. We are grateful for the concern of kindred spirits who share our love for the College and want it to stay the course."[27]

Grove City College's concern over what they saw as the danger of critical race theory exemplifies the fearful Christian university on several levels. First, "concerned alumni and friends" announce a threat to the university brand that requires response. Second, university power brokers (the trustees) step in to affirm the concerns of the critics and to cross the usually respected line between institutional governance and operational policy. Third, the crisis is in response to imagined and exaggerated threats from "the world." Fourth, the trustees are grateful to the concerned critics for keeping them on the straight and narrow. Finally, the trustees affirm their original preferred position without significantly engaging the reality behind the issue raised (in this case, how to talk about racial structures in society). In response to the special committee's report, Grove City eliminated diversity training for their student leaders, removed diversity classes from education requirements, and disbanded its diversity council. Nevertheless, a new student petition in 2022 complained that this response was insufficient because an adjunct faculty member wasn't fired and two departing student-life leaders were given "heroes' sendoffs."[28]

26. Grove City College Board of Trustees, "Report and Recommendation of the Special Committee," updated April 13, 2022, https://tinyurl.com/9xcu2nvx.
27. Grove City Board, "Report and Recommendation."
28. "Save Grove City," 2022, https://savegrovecity.com/about.

The Way Forward

Christian higher education needs to operate in a fearless manner. Fearless Christian universities would accept the internal and external shifts that have occurred and find ways of engaging those changes from a position of strength. They would be arguing for the special role they play in higher education. Students, faculty, and alumni would be seen as vast resources to shape a model of the Christian university that speaks into a pluralistic society in profound and important ways.

An initial step toward a new model is to reframe what we mean by a Christian university. Throughout my entire career in Christian higher education, it has seemed that the focus has been on *Christian*, with *higher education* a subordinate concern. I remember a regional CCCU leadership meeting where the standing president spoke to cabinet officers on "keeping the main thing the main thing." Of course, what he meant was Christian commitment. There was no conversation about pedagogy or curriculum.

What if we could instead articulate a vision of higher education that happens alongside Christian commitments? In other words, the main thing would be the educational process shaping students as they prepare for their futures. In no way would this shift diminish the Christian identity of the university; rather, it would put that identity in its proper place as a key component of the pedagogical mission of the institution.

A fearless Christian university would center its educational philosophy and practice within its Christian identity. Doing so would require a commitment to intellectual inquiry guided by epistemological humility. Recognizing that many issues are complex and represent diverse interests requires that the careful untangling of historical, contemporary, and emergent issues becomes a central part of the educational experience. A fearless approach emboldens faculty and students to engage ideas that seem foreign to the Christian worldview—not to dismiss them but first to understand them before any response is offered.[29]

29. I explore this in more depth in chapter 3.

Such an approach to Christian higher education is not novel. In fact, as Will Bunch shows in *After the Ivory Tower Falls*, the Truman Commission articulated just such a vision for higher education in the 1940s.[30] Educational experts Wendy Fischman and Howard Gardner conducted research of (non-Christian) institutions and discovered a significant minority of students committed to expanding what they called "Higher Education Capital."[31]

Most of the issues that trouble trustees, alumni, and donors—evolution, race, LGBTQ+ rights, gender, politics—could be managed by foregrounding the pedagogical commitments to pursue truth amid complexity.[32] Outside speakers who challenge the comfort level of the community could be the basis for further discussion with faculty, staff, and students. Seeing students move from short-term personal career goals to commitments to engage the broader world is a positive.[33]

How do we begin such a transition? I always come back to Parker Palmer's *The Courage to Teach*.[34] Palmer's Christian and spiritual commitments are evident throughout this classic written for a broad audience of educators. His approach to faithful teaching has shaped generations of educators at all levels, from elementary school through graduate school.

---

30. Will Bunch, *After the Ivory Tower Falls: How College Broke the American Dream and Blew Up Our Politics—and How to Fix It* (New York: William Morrow, 2022).

31. Wendy Fischman and Howard Gardner, *The Real World of College: What Higher Education Is and What It Can Be* (Cambridge, MA: The MIT Press, 2022).

32. At one institution I served, I argued for including an educational philosophy web page close to the university's landing page. I suggested that whenever a parent or trustee complained about a class or outside speaker, we could simply point to the web page as an explanation instead of legitimizing the concern voiced. Needless to say, my suggestion was not adopted.

33. In their mission statements, Christian universities typically express a desire to engage the broader world, but most lack the pedagogical commitments to make that happen. I take up this point in the next two chapters.

34. Parker J. Palmer, *The Courage to Teach: Exploring the Inner Landscape of a Teacher's Life*, 20th anniversary ed. (San Francisco: Jossey-Bass, 2017).

There's a particular passage where Palmer's spiritual voice comes through. It deals directly with the fear that too often constrains teachers and, as I argue in this book, entire institutions. He points out that one of the most common commands in many faith traditions is "Be not afraid."[35]

Palmer says that we should take this phrase literally: "Don't be the fear." Instead, we should acknowledge the fear but not allow it to define us. Once a fear is externalized, action in the face of it is possible. When we focus on fear, he says, it cuts off connectedness. Paradoxically, he argues that connectedness allows us to set aside fear.

This is what a fearless Christian university does. It recognizes that addressing social change or hearing students' concerns or living in true community is scary. Yet that fear does not get the last word. It is but the beginning of a liberating journey that truly engages the culture and stakes out a unique role for the Christian university in the sphere of higher education.

35. Palmer, *Courage to Teach*, 58–60.

Reimagining the Christian University Mission

It seems self-evident that the mission of an institution of higher education should be about teaching and learning. Nevertheless, understanding what a university mission statement is and how it is supposed to inform the life of an institution requires serious examination.

The guiding principles in the official mission statement should directly shape an institution's pedagogical and cocurricular components. However, in too many cases the mission statement has simply been adopted by the trustees, printed in the catalog, and put on plaques across campus. Beyond that, serious conversations about what the words in the statement might imply are few and far between. While this condition requires remedy throughout higher education, the need is particularly acute among Christian universities.

A university mission is so central that it constitutes the number one priority of accrediting bodies. Their standards for accreditation presume the centrality of mission and that it will inform all other aspects of the institution.[1] Consider how the Higher Learning Commission states its expectations for institutions of higher learning. Its first criteria for accreditation reads, "The institution's mission is clear and articulated publicly; it guides the institution's operations." It goes on to articulate components of this expectation: that the mission is communicated and operationalized, that it demonstrates a commitment to

---

1. I have served as an accreditation peer reviewer since 2002.

the common good, and that it provides opportunities for engagement in a diverse world.[2]

This focus on mission is key to understanding how accrediting bodies approach institutions. It doesn't matter whether the university in question is a major state university or a small Christian liberal arts college. Mission is the driver of the review. For institutions of all types, mission should be key to life within the university. That also means that the Christian liberal arts college won't be judged in comparison to the major research university. Each will be judged according to its own distinct mission.

In their excellent book *The Real World of College*,[3] Harvard educators Wendy Fischman and Howard Gardner explore the unique character of the nonvocational mission of the university experience. They aren't suggesting that future employment is irrelevant to the university and its students. They argue rather that we must understand the college experience primarily in educational terms during the college years. In their inductive study of nearly a dozen institutions of higher education over the course of a decade, they found that most students were unaware of the crucial assumptions driving their educational experience. They explain: "But left to its own devices, the mission [of a university] can come to seem an occasion for lip service, if not increasingly vestigial. And so, we emphatically embrace a practice that we term *intertwining*. Since, as we have argued, the only major legitimate purpose of an avowedly nonvocational college is an academic one, any additional mission needs to be carefully and thoroughly intertwined with the academic mission."[4]

It seems important, then, to explore how Christian universities define themselves in their mission statements. Understanding that self-definition is necessary before we can talk about how a fearless

2. Higher Learning Commission, "Criteria for Accreditation," 2022, https://tinyurl.com/2rkyj2fw.

3. Wendy Fischman and Howard Gardner, *The Real World of College: What Higher Education Is and What It Can Be* (Cambridge, MA: MIT Press, 2022).

4. Fischman and Gardner, *Real World*, 255–56.

Christian university might embrace that mission, align it within its operational life, and communicate that to the outside world—especially to the church.[5]

David McKenna, president of two Christian colleges and a seminary over the course of his career, was instrumental in creating a dialogue within the nascent Christian college movement. Through what became known as the Christian College Consortium (a forerunner of the CCCU), he suggested that "the integration of faith and learning" should be key to how Christian universities distinguish themselves.[6]

I mentioned this phrase in the previous chapter and want to unpack it a bit here. There was an assumption that "secular" institutions were deficient because they neglected the spiritual development and character formation components of a university education. In the Christian university, then, these two things would be brought together. Moreover, the faith component would infuse the learning component in ways that made Christian university pedagogically unique.

I have long argued that this separation is at odds with how learning actually occurs. If we examine how students incorporate information, we find that they do so in scaffolded fashion, building upon prior understandings and making modifications in light of new information or experiences. I'll return to this in the following chapter.

An Analysis of Mission Statements

I reviewed official mission statements from thirty Christian higher education institutions. Some of these are among the largest members of the CCCU. Some I included because they have a national reputa-

---

5. This latter point is the focus in chapter 8.

6. David L. McKenna, *Christ-Centered Higher Education: Memory, Meaning, and Momentum for the Twenty-First Century* (Eugene, OR: Cascade Books, 2012).

tion or have been in the news. A few I included because they left the CCCU in the middle of the last decade.[7]

Reviewing these thirty institutional mission statements gives some insight into how Christian universities differ from one another. Admittedly, these statements were developed by committee and may have been approved by the university community and trustees decades ago. And yet they provide clues as to the university's priorities through what they highlight and what they tacitly assume.

I uncovered ten themes in these mission statements. Some statements include only one of those themes. Others manage as many as four. Here are the ten themes: (1) Christian community, (2) Christ-centered, (3) holistic education, (4) academic excellence, (5) faith and learning integration, (6) faith and character development, (7) biblical foundations, (8) denominational identity, (9) separation from the secular world, and (10) graduate impact on church and society. I then grouped the themes into categories by affinity: institutional character (themes 1–3), educational characteristics (themes 4–6), external referent (themes 7–9), and future (theme 10).

Christian community was included in eight of the mission statements. This theme identifies the ways in which the campus provides the embodiment of Christians gathered together for a common educational purpose.

Christ-centered was mentioned by four institutions. This language is common in CCCU schools and serves to distinguish these institutions from loosely religious schools. The latter may once have had solid theological commitments, but these are now seen as merely historical by the institution. With the former, the ways this Christ-centeredness is fleshed out in institutional practice is not exactly clear.

Holistic education showed up six times. These schools included references to academics, spiritual life, and social life as components of education at their institution.

7. This happened after two Mennonite schools allowed LGBTQ+ employees. Other schools left because the CCCU wasn't harsher in dismissing these schools from membership. More on this in chapter 4.

Academic excellence (sometimes identified as "excellence in education") got five mentions. The former phrase stands as a commitment of all community members. The latter phrase identifies excellence in instruction without making explicit assumptions about students.

Faith and learning integration was described earlier as a key component of CCCU schools, and so it is not surprising that it shows up in mission statements. Three institutions specifically used the phrase in their statement.

Faith and character development was the second most mentioned theme, showing up fourteen times out of thirty schools. The idea here is that one of the primary tasks of the Christian university is to ensure that students are nurtured in faith and become people of integrity during their years on campus.

Biblical foundations was mentioned in eight statements. This total includes references to "biblically centered" education or "biblical submission." One assumes that these schools, by giving the Bible primacy over other authorities, will have an academic philosophy distinct from that of other institutions.

Denominational identity was mentioned five times. The institution made explicit reference to either its denominational parent or its broad theological tradition (e.g., Wesleyan). That doesn't mean that other institutions are independent of denominational groups. Far from it. But one supposes a difference between those schools that make their denominational affiliation part of their mission statement and those that leave it more implicit. As the percentage of students from the denominational sponsor drops, and these are replaced by students of more generic Christian faith or no faith at all, this distinguishing mark will be harder to maintain.

Separation from the secular world showed up in two statements. One of these specifically sets the institution in opposition to a "secular worldview." The other mentions "taking the Gospel to the World." The approach of a particular president's term might become far more antagonistic toward the broader society.[8] Additional statements of

8. This might be the case at Oklahoma Wesleyan, where the previous

value buried in the institution's strategic planning documents may show separation as an institutional value even if it's not mentioned in the mission statement.[9]

Graduate impact on church and society was the most common idea. Nineteen institutions made some explicit reference to how their graduates should affect the broader world through leadership in church or the broader society. Some mentioned "servant leadership" as a similar orientation. What leadership or servant leadership or "being Christ's agents" means is left undefined. One might also wonder what their attempts to fulfill this aim look like in practice.

In terms of the four broad categories, the largest share of mentions fell in the *educational characteristics* category, with 32 percent. The *future* orientation was second, at 25 percent. *Institutional characteristics* was just behind at 24 percent, with the *external referent* category at 19 percent.

What does this review of Christian university mission statements tell us? First, it underscores the tensions at play within the institutions. Academic priorities lead in one direction, while denominational commitments or methods of biblical interpretation might lead in another. The focus on internal community and the development of faith and character can be hard to reconcile with engaging and affecting the broader culture, because the former tends toward homogeneity and the latter toward diversity. The integration of faith and learning can lead to unsettling conclusions that denominational leaders might disagree with.

---

president was an opinion writer and prolific social media attack dog. Reviewing the web page suggests that the new president might not be quite as much of a separatist.

9. Colorado Christian's *Here We Stand* document lists the following among its strategic values: "impact our culture in support of traditional family values, sanctity of life, compassion for the poor, Biblical view of human nature, limited government, personal freedom, free markets, natural law, original intent of the Constitution, and Western Civilization" (7). Colorado Christian University, "*Here We Stand* Is a Deeper Look at What Makes CCU 'Unapologetically Christian,'" https://www.ccu.edu/about/here-we-stand/.

Second, many of the concepts described above may seem foreign to those outside the Christian university. While most people have a sense of what campus community, academic excellence, and future leadership mean, it may be quite a challenge for employers, grad schools, and the media to grasp what is meant by "Christ-centered" or "faith development" (to say nothing of "secular worldview"). This insider vocabulary marginalizes Christian universities at a time when they fear persecution and need much more support from the broader culture.

Third, what students know about—or whether they even care about—the mission statement is an open question.[10] Some institutions go to great lengths to have students be able to quote the mission statement by rote. Even if students have memorized the mission statement, they may really be attending because it lets them play soccer or be in musicals or live close to home. They haven't necessarily come *because of* the mission statement.

Fourth, different constituencies of the Christian university may emphasize different parts of the mission statement. What a college trustee means by the integration of faith and learning may differ sharply from what a psychology professor takes it to mean. What the student activities director thinks Christian community means might conflict with the chaplain's understanding. What the president means by Christ-centered can differ greatly from a theology professor's view of the same.[11]

There is nothing particularly wrong with most of the mission themes described here. What is missing is focus. Which of these themes

10. This is a particular challenge for homeschooled students. Because their prior education was fused with parental authority, they may be less aware of the range of educational philosophies.

11. My book for students entering a Christian university included a chapter using the four companions in *The Wizard of Oz* as metaphors for the roles of faculty, student development officials, administrators, and students. John W. Hawthorne, *A First Step into a Much Larger World: The Christian University and Beyond* (Eugene, OR: Wipf and Stock, 2014).

are central to the work of the Christian university, and which are better considered as the milieu or context in which that work takes place?

The most common theme above involves what students do after they graduate. This is important, but it doesn't clearly define what they do while they are enrolled. The second common theme was faith and character development. Again, this is part of the mission, but much of this work, except for required Bible or theology classes, takes place outside the classroom (in student life, in chapel, through special speakers). Christian community is an important component of the fearless Christian university, and not simply the setting in which the mission takes place.

A Bolder Mission

The academic enterprise should be at the heart of the fearless Christian university mission. Former Taylor University provost and current Gordon College president Michael Hammond, reflecting on the challenges facing Christian universities, suggested that there is now

> an opportunity to reassert the high place of learning in the evangelical movement. This movement originally saw education as a key to social activism, and Christian higher education is vital to leading this conversation. Postwar evangelicalism promoted Christian colleges, and the CCCU currently represents the network of institutions that are joined by a similar mission. Yet, politics has become more of the public face of evangelicalism. Christian colleges must now be clear about the theology, practices, values, and motives of the institution to build a better society for all. In today's culture, evangelicalism risks being misinterpreted or aligned with a political or cultural movement that may not be consistent with the institutional mission.[12]

12. Michael D. Hammond, "Christian Higher Education in the United States: The Crisis of Evangelical Identity," *Christian Higher Education* 18, no. 1–2 (2019): 3–15.

If, as Hammond suggests, Christian universities are to center their mission on the "high place of learning," much more work is necessary in conceptualizing exactly what that would imply.

Laurie Schreiner, director of the Azusa Pacific University doctoral program in higher education and coeditor of the *Journal of Christian Higher Education*, used data from the National Study of Student Engagement to examine learning in Christian universities as reported by nearly 15,000 students. She found something of a mixed bag when it came to student learning. On the one hand, 83 percent of seniors reported that courses in their major helped them think about the exercise of Christian values in their field. That was, however, only a 7 percent gain over the same question answered by freshmen (she points out that this was a cross-sectional survey, so longitudinal data would be better).[13] In another analysis, she compared the learning activities of CCCU seniors with those of seniors at other private institutions. The results show minimal differences between the two sets of seniors.[14]

Centering the Student Experience

To begin to unpack what it might look like to put academic experience at the center of the Christian university mission, we can return to the work of Fischman and Gardner.[15] As they approached their interviews with students, they had proposed four models of college learning. One of these they labeled inertial, which treats college as an unreflective next step in the educational journey. Thankfully, a very small number of students aligned with this approach. Another approach is what they called exploratory. This is where students take a variety of courses and are exposed to lots of ideas, but little synthesis takes place. The third is transactional, which sees all coursework as part of

13. Laurie A. Schreiner, "What Good Is Christian Higher Education?," *Christian Higher Education* 17, no. 1–2 (2018): 39.

14. Schreiner, "What Good," 44.

15. Fischman and Gardner, *Real World*, ch. 5.

the pursuit of a credential that will result in satisfactory employment. The fourth is transformational, where the student incorporates new learning into a deeper and richer synthesis of understanding oneself and the broader world.

These approaches to learning connect to another set of ideas they lay out in the book, the development of Higher Education Capital (HEDCAP) mentioned in the previous chapter.[16] To them, HED-CAP "denotes the ability to attend, analyze, reflect, connect, and communicate on issues of importance and interest."[17] They find that about a third of seniors showed high HEDCAP levels, roughly twice that of freshmen (again, not longitudinal). When controlling for the selectivity of schools, they find high HEDCAP scores in 15 percent of students in low selectivity schools, which increases to 20 percent for medium selectivity and 36 percent for high selectivity institutions.[18]

There are two things to note in this data. First, most students in college are not achieving high HEDCAP scores. Second, most Christian universities fall in the medium selectivity category. If Fischman and Gardner are right in their thinking about the goals of higher education, and I think they are, then a fearless Christian university needs to seriously rethink its educational processes.

The college experience is built upon one of the great life-cycle transitions in a young person's life, perhaps exceeded only by the move from home to preschool or kindergarten. Throughout a student's first twelve years of education, school and home operate in tandem. One goes from home to school and back home. The (relative) stability of family life provides an anchor amid the ups and downs of school life.

Not so with college, at least for most students. Home and previous social relationships are pushed to the background, even while potentially linked via social media or text. Where one previously lived according to the rules of the house ("while you're under our roof"), now

16. Fischman and Gardner, *Real World*, ch. 4.
17. Fischman and Gardner, *Real World*, 79–80.
18. Fischman and Gardner, *Real World*, 102.

there is a tremendous sense of independence—even if that is somewhat bounded by a student handbook. The local church previously provided the context for what it means to be a Christian. Trusted pastors and youth pastors—often the only ones the student has known— are replaced by a campus chapel, decentralized Bible studies, and a diversity of religious views, even among Christian students.

Given the discontinuities created by this transition to college, it is not surprising that Jeffrey Jensen Arnett has defined it as the beginning of a unique developmental phase, emerging adulthood.[19] This phase, also experienced to some degree by those who don't attend college, runs from age eighteen to twenty-nine. Arnett identifies five features that characterize this phase: identity exploration, instability, self-focus, feeling in-between, and opportunity.

These five characteristics may be even more pronounced at Christian universities than at other colleges. Perhaps this is because home life was more proscribed for students at Christian universities, especially those who attended Christian high schools or, even more so, were homeschooled. Being away from home and living in a college residence hall requires a student to engage in a certain degree of individuation and identity reformation. Sometimes this takes the form of rule-breaking behavior (either home rules, campus rules, or both).[20] In nearly all cases, this new living situation provides a student the opportunity to explore new ideas and perspectives, ones that might not have been countenanced at home or church.

In addition to these very personal transitions, today's Christian university students have experienced unbelievable levels of social change. An eighteen-year-old freshman beginning at a Christian university in 2023 was not alive on 9/11. She was nine when Michael

19. Jeffrey Jensen Arnett, *Emerging Adulthood: The Winding Road from the Late Teens through the Twenties*, 2nd ed. (New York: Oxford University Press, 2015).

20. See Christian Smith, with Kari Christoffersen, Hilary Davidson, and Patricia Snell Herzog, *Lost in Transition: The Dark Side of Emerging Adulthood* (New York: Oxford University Press, 2011).

Brown was shot in Ferguson and ten when *Obergefell* was decided. She was eleven when Donald Trump was elected president. She was twelve when the Harvey Weinstein harassment case broke and thirteen when the Southern Baptist Church sexual abuse patterns became news. And all those events happened not in some faraway place reported on the evening news but on the daily social media feeds that were ubiquitous in her life.

When we consider the immense personal and social transitions today's Christian university students face, it becomes clear why the transformational model of education described by Fischman and Gardner is so important.[21] The transactional model is simply a focus on future job prospects. And the exploratory model involves taking lots of courses and meeting new people, but to what end? The transformational model, however, takes the exploration of diverse information as its raw material and delivers job prospects as a by-product of the educational journey. Fischman and Gardner define the transformational model as follows: "One goes to college to reflect about, and question, one's own values and beliefs, with the expectation, and often, as well, the aspiration that one may change in fundamental ways." This transformational approach to higher education is best paired with the development of Higher Education Capital, the ability to reflect upon and articulate one's views in light of changes over time and within the broader social context. Moreover, the requisite skills for doing this are generally not developed in secondary education, whether public, private, or homeschool.[22]

Centering the student's transformational journey requires addressing those issues that the trustees and administrators described in the previous chapter would rather avoid. Christian universities must allow questions about the role of race in American history, about gender dysphoria and sexual orientation, about the limits of science, about economic inequality, about abuse in the church arising from patriar-

21. Fischman and Gardner, *Real World*, 122.

22. As we saw earlier, exceptions can be found at highly selective institutions, but most Christian universities are not in this category.

chal views, about changing family structures, about our divided political landscape, and about many other matters. They must do so not because they are "woke" but because these are the very questions the students are seeking to answer.

This transformational mission is not limited to the classroom. The philosophy of the curriculum is important and will be addressed in the next chapter. But the transformational mission, as Fischman and Gardner argue, must cut across the full spectrum of the student experience.

Most of the mission statements described above are completely compatible with the transformational mission. They simply provide the context (Christian community, faith and character development), the method (holistic learning, faith and learning integration), or the outcome (graduate impact on church and society) of the fearless Christian university. Some of them (biblical foundations, denominational identity, separation) are more removed and require some unpacking, which I will undertake in chapter 4.

Here is a shorthand way to think about the difference between a fearful Christian university and a fearless Christian university. The former places the abstract notion of "the institution" or "the brand" above all else. Because this is so easily threatened from a myriad of sources, the university must be perpetually on guard.

On the other hand, a fearless Christian university is focused on what is happening with the students. Because the university is serving them on their journey to become what they feel called to be, there is no need for apology, regardless of who might complain.

CHAPTER THREE

Preparing Students for the Future

The thesis of Francis Schaeffer's best-selling 1976 book *How Should We Then Live?*[1] and the documentary series on which it was based was that the modern world, based on rationality and human effort, was so defiled that the social problems confronting society were but a natural result. Historian Molly Worthen summarized Schaeffer's impact as follows:

> Schaeffer wanted evangelical Americans to become soldiers of history rather than careful students. He was one of a wave of gurus who, like generations of prophets and big personalities before them, offered evangelicals an alternative authority, a rubric of certainty at a time when the consensus on the Bible's status in American culture was shakier than ever. While he inspired some young evangelicals to get to the bottom of the stories he told by pursuing graduate degrees in history and philosophy, on a larger scale Schaeffer's ministry was a grand and clever exercise in anti-intellectualism. He deployed the trappings of academic investigation—litanies of historical names and dates; an accommodating version of Enlightenment reasoning—to quash inquiry rather than encourage it, to mobilize his audiences rather than provoke them to ask questions.[2]

1. Francis Schaeffer, *How Should We Then Live? The Rise and Decline of Western Thought and Culture* (New York: Fleming Revell, 1976).
2. Molly Worthen, *Apostles of Reason: The Crisis of Authority in American Evangelicalism* (New York: Oxford University Press, 2014), 218–19.

We saw in the previous chapter that some Christian university mission statements include references to a "biblical worldview" or set themselves in contrast to the "secular world." And there is the ubiquitous "integration of faith and learning," suggesting that how education occurs at a Christian university must be markedly different from what happens at its secular counterpart down the road.

In 1999, evangelical leader Chuck Colson and apologist Nancy Pearcey outlined their own approach to the Christian worldview (borrowing heavily from Schaeffer).[3] Relying upon Reformed theology, they built upon the topics of creation, fall, redemption, and restoration as central to Christian understanding. More importantly, they contrasted these Christian concepts with "secular" concepts like autonomy, relativism, and scientism as a foil.

The result is a combination of an affirmative message about Christian theology and a negative message about the world at large. Early in the book, they argue the following: "Understanding Christianity as a total life system is absolutely essential, for two reasons. First, it enables us to make sense of the world we live in and thus order our lives more rationally. Second, it enables us to *understand forces hostile to our faith*, equipping us to evangelize and to defend Christian truth as God's instruments for transforming culture."[4]

Later, as they discuss the importance of schooling, we see the same twin images. This ambivalence shaped much of pedagogy in Christian higher education in the early part of this century, as Adam Laats has documented.[5] Colson and Pearcey continue: "Christian education is not simply a matter of starting class with Bible reading and prayer, then teaching subjects out of secular textbooks. It consists of teaching everything, from science and mathematics to literature and the arts, within the *framework of an integrated biblical worldview*. It means teaching students to relate every academic discipline to God's truth and his self-revelation

3. Charles Colson and Nancy Pearcey, *How Now Shall We Live?* (Carol Stream, IL: Tyndale House, 1999).

4. Colson and Pearcey, *How Now*, 44. Italics mine.

5. Adam Laats, *Fundamentalist U: Keeping the Faith in American Higher Education* (New York: Oxford University Press, 2018).

in Scripture, while detecting and critiquing nonbiblical worldview assumptions."[6] This distrust of the broader intellectual world—much like that expressed by Francis Schaeffer and Chuck Colson—is consistent with a common strategy in Christian universities of identifying what a Christian worldview looks like and teaching students its contours.

In 2002, David Dockery and others at Union University published *Shaping a Christian Worldview: The Foundations of Christian Higher Education*.[7] Dockery, Union's president at the time, solicited essays from a variety of Union faculty. Following a foreword from Chuck Colson, the book starts with a set of introductory framing essays and then moves into discipline-specific essays. In his introduction, Dockery writes:

> A Christian worldview is a coherent way of seeing life, of seeing the world *distinct from deism, naturalism, and materialism (whether in its Darwinistic, humanistic, or Marxist forms), existentialism, polytheism, pantheism, mysticism, or deconstructionist postmodernism.* Such a theistic perspective provides bearings and direction *when confronted with New Age spirituality or secularistic and pluralistic approaches to truth and morality.* Fear about the future, suffering, disease, and poverty are informed by a Christian worldview grounded in the redemptive work of Christ and the grandeur of God. *As opposed to the meaningless and purposeless nihilistic perspectives of F. Nietzsche, E. Hemingway, or J. Cage,* a Christian worldview offers meaning and purpose for all aspects of life.[8]

Notice the primary focus of this paragraph. It's not on the Christian worldview per se but on it as an alternative to all the other flawed approaches in the contemporary world.

6. Colson and Pearcey, *How Now*, 531. Italics mine.
7. David S. Dockery and Gregory Alan Thornbury, *Shaping a Christian Worldview: The Foundations of Christian Higher Education* (Nashville: Broadman & Holman, 2002).
8. Dockery and Thornbury, *Shaping a Christian Worldview*, 10. Italics mine.

This inherently distrustful approach to worldview is the Achilles' heel of Christian higher education. The idea of what ought to happen pedagogically inside the Christian university is underdeveloped because the focus is on what lies outside the institution.

There are several reasons why this approach is insufficient, at least without significant nuance. First, the student is too often a passive recipient of the contrasts between Christian and secular worldviews. They are too often introduced to presumedly non- or anti-Christian perspectives by the professor and then told how to refute those. It's not deep, genuine learning—true encounter and careful consideration—but a pro forma exercise that goes along with being in a Christian university. Once the student has graduated, it is quickly forgotten.

Second, the very toolkit used in critiquing secular perspectives becomes a model for how to examine implicit assumptions and interrogate alternatives. In her memoir *Evolving in Monkey Town*,[9] the late Rachel Held Evans states this well: "You might say that the apologetics movement created a monster. I'd gotten so good at critiquing all the fallacies of opposing worldviews, at searching for truth through objective analysis, that it was only a matter of time before I turned the same skeptical views upon my own faith."[10]

Similarly, Jonathan Merritt reflected on the apologetics approach of his youth and the ways in which it stilted his faith. In *Jesus Is Better Than You Imagined*,[11] he writes:

> My student pastor told me that I needed to read some apologetic books so I could argue better. I took his advice, rooting my faith in rationalism and relying on logic to help me solve faith's greatest questions. I began to explore all the "evidence that demands a verdict" and construct a "case for faith." While these efforts re-

9. Rachel Held Evans, *Evolving in Monkey Town: How a Girl Who Knew All the Answers Learned to Ask Questions* (Grand Rapids: Zondervan, 2010).
10. Evans, *Evolving in Monkey Town*, 79.
11. Jonathan Merritt, *Jesus Is Better Than You Imagined* (New York: Hachette Book Group, 2014).

minded me that my faith wasn't as silly as my skeptical friends seemed to believe, they failed to sustain me. I had boiled down the great depths of God and faith to arguments short enough to fit on an index card, easily memorized and ready to deploy in debates, and reduced my relationship with Jesus to a few bullet points to be shelved in my head and not worked out with my hands. My spirit thirsted for a supernatural encounter with a God who transcends logic.[12]

Third, because the Christian worldview is not integrated into the student's self-understanding those lessons may be easily discarded after they graduate and leave the supportive surrounds of the Christian university. Once outside, they are no longer thinking in these terms.

It reminds me of one of my favorite passages in Peter Berger's 1961 *Invitation to Sociology: A Humanistic Perspective*.[13] He has a fascinating section on what he calls "alternation":

Intensive occupation with the more fully elaborated meaning systems available in our time gives one a truly frightening understanding of the way in which these systems can provide a total interpretation of reality, within which will be included an interpretation of the alternate systems and of the ways of passing from one system to another. Catholicism may have a theory of Communism, but Communism returns the compliment and will produce a theory of Catholicism. To the Catholic thinker the Communist lives in a dark world of materialist delusion about the real meaning of life. To the Communist his Catholic adversary is helplessly caught in the "false consciousness" of a bourgeois mentality. To the psychoanalyst both Catholic and Communist may simply be acting out on the intellectual level the unconscious impulses that

12. Merritt, *Jesus Is Better*, 50.
13. Peter Berger, *Invitation to Sociology: A Humanistic Perspective* (New York: Doubleday, 1963).

really move them. And psychoanalysis may be to the Catholic an escape from the reality of sin and to the Communist an avoidance of the realities of society. This means that the individual's choice of viewpoint will determine the way in which he looks back upon his own biography.[14]

In place of a Christian worldview focus, I would much prefer an approach to Christian pedagogy that builds from the students' experience, coursework, career dreams, and faith toward a coherent whole. Such a coherence would certainly serve the students for a longer period of time than our current process, which allows them to drop all this once they graduate, if not before.

Fourth, faculty members have already navigated these waters as part of their professional journey. A Christian faculty member moving through graduate education must decide what to exclude from the repertoire, what to reinterpret, what to accept. To ask faculty to rail at the latest boogeyman will incite them to perform before their students rather than truly engage with them and the material under consideration. Furthermore, modeling Christian intellectual character is key to developing the inquisitiveness desired in students as they go on to become life-long learners affecting society.[15] It is noteworthy that two contributors to the introductory section of the Dockery book have personally told me that the worldview focus was a mistake.

Worldview approaches work deductively. They attempt to persuade students of the right answers without considering the questions arising from their experiences. They are prepared to describe what is wrong with a particular secular view, but that doesn't help them with the inductive task of making sense of their lived experience.

So, is there a single Christian worldview that motivates Christian higher education? Probably not. There is instead a multitude of Christian perspectives brought to the university from students' family,

14. Berger, *Invitation to Sociology*, 52.
15. This is Fischman and Gardner's Higher Education Capital, mentioned earlier.

church, or private school experiences. Rather than layering on a tri-
umphalist set of beliefs showing why Christianity is better than other
philosophical systems, what is needed is a pedagogy that will help
students find their own path as thoughtful Christians ready to engage
the broader culture.

This latter approach requires not more classes on Christian thought
but a focus on how the individual student navigates the college experience. In place of Christian worldview training, we need a pedagogy
that helps students internalize their faith and their learning—not as
two distinct things that must be forced together but as a coherent
whole that can face up to whatever crises may arise in the world.

Shifting Worldviews

Throughout his career, sociologist James Davison Hunter has focused
on the idea of evangelicalism as a cultural system.[16] The critical challenge he identified in his 1983 book, *American Evangelicalism*, is holding together a coherent set of ideas regarding theology, society, and
practice in the face of the massive cultural changes as modernity shifts
into postmodernity.

Hunter's concern for what he calls "the quandary of modernity" remains with us today. In *American Evangelicalism*, he lays out the challenge:

> The adherents of a religious world view may either attempt to
> resist the compromising realities of modernity or attempt to make
> the best of the situation by giving in to modernity's cognitive

16. James Davison Hunter, *American Evangelicalism: Conservative Religion
and the Quandary of Modernity* (New Brunswick, NJ: Rutgers University
Press, 1983); James Davison Hunter, *Evangelicals: The Coming Generation*
(Chicago: University of Chicago Press, 1987); James Davison Hunter, *To
Change the World: The Irony, Tragedy, and Possibility of Christianity in the Late
Modern World* (New York: Oxford University Press, 2010).

pressures. Of course there is between these two ideals a continuum of possibility on which most empirical cases lie. In any case, however, a fundamental premise here is that there is a constant casual reciprocity between consciousness and social structure and therefore that interaction between religious world views and the structures and processes of modernity will be a sociological necessity. At the level of consciousness, the dynamics of this interaction may be labeled *cognitive bargaining*.[17]

Hunter's cognitive bargaining should be at the center of all pedagogy in Christian higher education. Given that students have experienced tremendous social change in their short lifetimes and that they will experience far more in the decades to come, they must develop skills, attitudes, and behaviors that put that cognitive bargaining to work—not just during their time at college but for a lifetime. It is to that pedagogical challenge we now turn.

Plausibility Structures

Students who come to Christian university from homes with a significant investment in Christian infrastructure (youth group, retreats, Bible studies, support groups) approach their faith within the context of what Peter Berger called a "plausibility structure."[18] Consider a plausibility structure to be a set of social structures that inculcate and support, by tacit in-group agreement, a particular set of ideas about faith, society, and the world.

How well those structures are internalized can vary. The more the religious perspective of church and family is threatened by the surrounding culture, the more likely that perspective is closed off to

17. Hunter, *American Evangelicalism*, 15. Italics original.
18. Peter Berger, *The Sacred Canopy: Elements of a Sociological Theory of Religion* (Garden City, NY: Doubleday, 1967).

outside influences.[19] A student whose pre-college years were spent in Christian schools will struggle more with matters that threaten the prior understandings of home and church. For homeschooled students, this sense of dissonance is heightened even further. On the other hand, students who come to a Christian university with a less developed cognitive framework will have a lessened subjective sense of religious plausibility.

A Substack newsletter from D. L. Mayfield illustrates how a more rigid cognitive framework was shaped during Mayfield's adolescent years.[20] Growing up steeped in white evangelical subculture of the 1980s, Mayfield reflects on the totalizing effect of that subculture:

> I truly believe there was a generational shift in conservative, white religious communities that happened in the 70s, 80s, and 90s, leading to an unprecedented amount of cultural artifacts and media that were all aimed at indoctrinating children and teenagers. The white evangelical indoctrination station, we can call it. And I've spent the past few years/decades of my life trying to interrogate these artifacts. Do you remember any of them?
>
> Here are just a few examples:
>
> Adventures in Odyssey, the Strong-Willed Child, Jesus Freak, Brio Magazine, Frank Peretti, Focus on the Family magazine, Christianity Today, I Kissed Dating Goodbye, the Prayer of Jabez, Chicken Soup for the Soul, Touched by an Angel, the Left Behind Series, Acquire the Fire, Passion, Billy Graham, Hell Houses, Youth Group, Dare to Discipline, Wayne Grudem's Systematic Theology, Harvest Parties, John Piper, McGee and Me, Veggie Tales, Conversion Therapy, Y2k prophecies, Francis Chan, Mission trips, Bible studies, Bible colleges, Campus Crusade for Christ, Intervarsity, WOW CDs, Promise Keeper's, Francine Rivers, Max Lucado Bibles, Missions week, purity rings, Elizabeth Elliot, World Vision, and more.

19. David John Seel, *The New Copernicans* (Nashville: Thomas Nelson, 2018).
20. D. L. Mayfield, "Deconversion: Part 1," *Healing Is My Special Interest*, Substack, January 3, 2023, https://dlmayfield.substack.com/p/deconversion-part-1.

The problem for Mayfield, like a great many more of the same generation, is that these artificial structures promoting a particular worldview were insufficient for the challenges of adult life. Mayfield's memoir documents the struggles of attempting to reconceptualize one's faith in light of lived experience.[21]

This process of dismantling one's prior weaker cognitive framework in order to build a more robust one that reflects a true subjective understanding of faith and learning is known as deconstruction. While critics will demean this process as a search for permission to abandon the faith,[22] those who have looked more carefully at the process see it as a healthy adaptation to Hunter's cognitive bargaining.

A review of social media feeds and blog posts around deconstruction shows a consistent pattern among millennials and early Gen Zs. Yet one can also find faithful older Christians who have played key roles in supporting worldview thinking now exploring how to reimagine their early religious life in a more vibrant contemporary state.[23]

For far too many, the deconstruction they undertake in their thirties or beyond proves to be a major crisis. In Berger's terms, it requires one to come to terms with a fragile plausibility structure. Too often, the solution is to abandon the faith altogether. Frankly, the evangelical church often left them unprepared for the potential faith crises that lay in their path.

Every Christian university student will go through some aspects of deconstruction. Some of that occurs with the shift in location from home and church to the college environment. Some occurs when students must confront the diversity of thought present among their peers, even though most of them may come from Christian

---

21. D. L. Mayfield, *Assimilate or Go Home: Notes from a Failed Missionary on Rediscovering Faith* (New York: HarperCollins, 2016).

22. Or, more cynically, they may argue that the individual just wants to engage in premarital sex without judgment.

23. See David P. Gushee, *After Evangelicalism: The Path to a New Christianity* (Louisville: Westminster John Knox Press, 2020); Philip Yancey, *Where the Light Fell* (New York: Convergent Publishing, 2021).

backgrounds. For still others, it will be the challenge of reconciling the differing views of two favorite professors. For yet others, it will come after graduation as they attempt to reconcile the world they're living in with the somewhat rigid Christian environments they've left behind.

PREPARING FOR THE FUTURE

Somewhat ironically, then, the pedagogical focus of Christian higher education should focus on preparing students for the ongoing and future challenges of deconstruction as opposed to maintaining institutionally defined worldviews. If the end goal is to send Christian graduates into the world, then the student experience must take precedence over the institutional view. To put it in Berger's terms, if the subjective plausibility structure is to thrive, it needs key processes and practices that will allow it to develop.

I can paint a picture of some key assumptions that might drive our pedagogy. This requires a more careful unpacking of the phrase *integration of faith and learning* so familiar to Christian higher education.[24]

Let's begin with faith, as this is what Christian universities lead with. Far too many students, even those entering a Christian institution, have a very rudimentary understanding of the Bible and theology. They have been shaped by youth groups and summer camps and "see you at the pole."[25] They are quite likely to see their home church as *the* church, perhaps hearing sermons from only one or two pastors throughout their youth.

This leads to a vague familiarity with faith combined with personal passion. Barbara Brown Taylor describes the challenge faced

24. Another ubiquitous phrase that could do with some careful unpacking is "All truth is God's truth."

25. Kenda Creasy Dean, *Almost Christian: What the Faith of Our Teenagers Is Telling the American Church* (New York: Oxford University Press, 2010); Melinda Lundquist Denton and Richard Flory, *Back-Pocket God: Religion and Spirituality in the Lives of Emerging Adults* (New York: Oxford University Press, 2020).

by a student in her World Religions course at a mid-sized Southern liberal arts college:

> As she speaks, I imagine her in front of her mental file cabinet with her class notes in her hand. The labels on the drawers say, "Sunday School" "Bible Study" "Youth Group" and "Personal Relationship with Christ." Those drawers hold important, life-giving things, but where is she supposed to put her new insight about the role of the early churches in the formation of the New Testament? Where does she put her new awareness of the Eastern Orthodox Church? The problem is not that her drawers are full. The problem is that none of the labels on them match what is in her hand.[26]

A teenage passion for Jesus is important but is somewhat untethered from broader understandings of the Bible and theology. It reflects the practices of the Christian life that D. L. Mayfield was discussing. It can be seen in the Christian subculture of students in a public high school.[27] This passion is also evident in the buoyant enthusiasm of freshmen in a Christian college chapel, which sometimes wears off by the junior year.

Critics will point to this apparent waning of passion as evidence that higher education has a secularizing impact even at a Christian school. But the passion isn't necessarily gone. It may have deepened and become more of a core part of the student's identity than an outward display of faith ever was. It is exactly what should happen. And it's going to happen again and again.

Each conversation with a new roommate, every job internship, a new class outside one's normal studies, a change in family life through divorce or death, graduation, finding oneself in a new city and a brand-new job, getting married, having children—any and all of these may prompt a significant re-formation of faith. The Christian university is

26. Barbara Brown Taylor, *Holy Envy: Finding God in the Faith of Others* (New York: HarperOne, 2019), 140.

27. Addie Zierman, *When We Were on Fire: A Memoir of Consuming Faith, Tangled Love, and Starting Over* (New York: Convergent Books, 2013).

hewing to its mission when these life events and changes deepen the faith of its students.

Christian higher education need not rely on Bible quotes or prayer before class to form deeply ingrained faith in students. Instead, students are open to exploring with faculty the implications of various academic fields for reconceptualizing and deepening faith.

Peter Enns, a professor of biblical studies at Eastern University, aptly illustrates how this process has worked in his own life in *Curveball*.[28] He describes the ways in which his tidy faith had to be stretched and reworked as he processed various discoveries and events.

Two of these stand out in the book. First, he considers how our scientific discoveries in cosmology affected his human-and-earth–centered faith. As an Old Testament scholar, he was well-versed in the ways those in the ancient Near East understood God as the center and sustainer of their universe (in the limited way they understood it). But looking through the lens of the James Webb Space Telescope, we see galaxies upon galaxies. What does all that vastness mean for our very parochial understandings of the relationship between God and humans? One option is to bifurcate one's understanding of the size of the universe and one's biblical commitments. But mature and deep faith doesn't do that. Instead, it wrestles. Enns writes: "In our time, our understanding of the world and the universe has changed more dramatically and more quickly than at any other time in human history. Such rapid changes can understandably make us feel nervous and want to cling more tightly to familiar ways of thinking about God. But it is precisely because of these rapid and fundamental changes to our understanding of reality that I feel I need to adjust my understanding of God to keep pace."[29]

If the vast size of the universe requires rethinking prior faith commitments, so does the infinitesimally small world of quantum mechanics. After reviewing how scientists think photons work and exploring the mysteries of how photons interact with each other at the subatomic

28. Peter Enns, *Curveball: When Your Faith Takes Turns You Never Saw Coming (or, How I Stumbled and Tripped My Way to Finding a Bigger God)* (New York: HarperOne, 2023).

29. Enns, *Curveball*, 95.

level, Enns recognizes that relationality seems to be key to how pro-
tons operate. Returning to considering heavenly bodies, he observes
relationality there as well in terms of gravitational fields and planetary
orbits. Where does one find faith in the midst of things so tiny and so
huge? Enns writes: "A God who encompasses the infinitely large and
infinitely small must truly be Spirit—though even that image might
suggest an 'entity' floating about. As Spirit, it seems to me, God is
not simply a big 'thing' that is everywhere at once, but woven in and
through all of reality—all matter. The best way for me to think about
God at the moment is as vibrantly, energetically present in creation,
from the inside out."[30] So rather than falling back on easy proof-text
verses from Sunday School, we are instead drawn to one of the great
confessions of deep faith from the book of Colossians: "Everything was
created by him, everything in heaven and on earth, including all forces
and powers, and all rulers and authorities. All things were created by
God's Son, and everything was made for him. God's Son was before
all else, and by him everything is held together" (1:16–17 CEV).

It's important to underscore that Pete Enns isn't twenty years old.
This level of reflection takes decades to work out. But it is crucially
important that Christian universities provide students with tools and
experiences that will allow them to begin this lifelong journey. To go
back to Barbara Brown Taylor's story, we must give them labels that
affirm their journey.

Failure to do so sets students up for future challenges when they
cannot reconcile their earlier faith with their new experiences. These are
nearly guaranteed to occur at regular intervals in life. Those who identify as "exvangelicals" illustrate common challenges. Their prior cognitive frameworks were not sufficiently pliable to allow them to adjust to
new discoveries or information. Too often they blame the faith itself
rather than the changes they confront through their experiences.

Knowing that potential faith challenges will present themselves in
every student's future life, the Christian university should commit itself to what I will call "anticipatory deconstruction." Because we know
that some crisis or other awaits them, we are preparing students to

30. Enns, *Curveball*, 155.

identify it when it comes and to marshal the resources necessary to keep their faith flexible enough to process it.

From the time a student is being recruited, she should be aware that her faith will be tested, refined, and developed. At this university, chapel addresses will expose her to thinkers that stretch her current perspectives rather than affirm her prior ideas. Guest lectures will invite notable alumni, not just to talk about their current work or to reminisce about their happy college days but to give testimony to their real faith struggles as they moved beyond the university. Faculty members will speak openly of the challenges presented by their subject material and how they reconciled those challenges in a deepened faith.[31] Administrators will celebrate the uncertainties of the age and show how faith can incorporate those uncertainties rather than simply denounce them. Trustees will celebrate the journey she is on and provide funding for new experiences that will test her faith to make it stronger.[32] Graduation will literally be a pause in her journey, celebrating the faith that has been nurtured so far and affirming the presence of the skills and aptitudes that will carry her into an unknown future.

Rather than try to keep student learning constrained by a Christian worldview, with its antagonism toward the surrounding culture, we instead prepare students for how to thrive in that culture as an act of faith. This, then, is the central task of the fearless Christian university: to nurture in students a holistic faith that confidently takes up all of life's experiences—in the classroom, in the dorm room, in chapel, at the internship, when studying abroad, in their jobs—to build a relational model where "everything is held together."

31. As a sociologist, I had to struggle over what to do with Marx's atheism and how to separate his social and economic analysis from his distance from faith.

32. More on this in chapter 7.

On Not Fighting Culture Wars

The Supreme Court of the United States ruled in June of 2020 that employment discrimination against gay employees violated Title VII of the Civil Rights Act. The decision, known as *Bostock v. Clayton County*, was a six to three decision written by Justice Gorsuch with support from Chief Justice Roberts and Justices Ginsburg, Sotomayor, Kagan, and Breyer.[1] Justices Alito, Kavanaugh, and Thomas dissented. The majority's summary reads:

> An employer violates Title VII when it intentionally fires an individual employee based in part on sex. It makes no difference if other factors besides the plaintiff's sex contributed to the decision or that the employer treated women as a group the same when compared to men as a group. A statutory violation occurs if an employer intentionally relies in part on an individual employee's sex when deciding to discharge the employee. Because discrimination on the basis of homosexuality or transgender status requires an employer to intentionally treat individual employees differently because of their sex, an employer who intentionally penalizes an employee for being homosexual or transgender also violates Title VII. There is no escaping the role intent plays: Just as sex is necessarily a but-for cause when an employer discriminates

---

1. Bostock v. Clayton County, Georgia, 590 U.S. ___, 140 S. Ct. 1731 (2020), https://tinyurl.com/bdeeeydm.

against homosexual or transgender employees, an employer who discriminates on these grounds inescapably intends to rely on sex in its decision making.

In April of 2021, the College of the Ozarks, a Christian university in Point Lookout, Missouri, sued the new Biden administration and the Department of Housing and Urban Development (HUD), arguing that any new rules following *Bostock* would violate the school's religious freedom.[2] With the aid of the Alliance Defending Freedom, they sought injunctive relief to block HUD from any requirements for changes to the college's dormitory policies.

The district court dismissed the case in May 2021, arguing that the college lacked standing because it couldn't demonstrate actual harm.[3] The college appealed the ruling to the Eighth Circuit Court of Appeals, which denied the appeal in July 2022.[4] Of particular note is this paragraph from the appellate decision: "*Allegedly fearing that its housing policies are now unlawful* under the Memorandum's interpretation of the Fair Housing Act, the College sued President Biden, the Department of HUD, the Secretary of HUD, and the Acting Assistant Secretary, seeking pre-enforcement review of the Memorandum. The complaint alleged that the Memorandum, among other things, violates the Administrative Procedure Act, the First Amendment's Free Speech and Free Exercise Clauses, the Appointments Clause of Article II of the Constitution, and the Religious Freedom Restoration Act."[5]

2. The complaint the Alliance Defending Freedom brought against Biden et al. on behalf of the College of the Ozarks in July 2021 can be viewed at https://tinyurl.com/47ejbedz.

3. "Request Denied as College of the Ozarks Challenges Biden Administration over Gender Identity Directive," KY3, May 23, 2021, https://tinyurl.com/5yztpxr5.

4. Scott Jaschik, "Appeals Court Rejects Suit by College of the Ozarks," *Inside Higher Ed*, July 27, 2022, https://tinyurl.com/yptyjkpv.

5. The School of the Ozarks, Inc., dba College of the Ozarks, Petitioner,

This sense of fear drives too much of Christian higher education. There is a default assumption that the government is taking an antagonistic stance toward the Christian university and must be regularly confronted, even if—as is the case with College of the Ozarks—there was no attempt to enforce federal policy on Christian institutions. This fear has a long history, and it has been kept alive by a variety of entities who thrive on its existence. As we will see, it is often counterproductive.

Historian Randall Balmer has been a leader in exploring the myriad ways in which federal action denying tax-exempt status to Bob Jones University in the 1970s and 1980s led to the creation of the Moral Majority.[6] Bob Jones had long had a policy banning and then limiting the admission of students of color. The government argued that this violated the Civil Rights Act and removed the institution's tax-exempt status and their Title IV eligibility (supporting federal student grants and loans). Bob Jones University pushed back, claiming that this was no simple policy disagreement but a direct infringement of its religious freedom.

This move shifted what was a public policy disagreement into religious freedom terms. Numerous institutions over the years have followed this road map. In *Bad Faith*, Balmer makes the case that conservative activists saw an opportunity to use the religious freedom claims to build a movement. He reports:

> As Bob Jones University sued to retain its tax exemption, [Paul] Weyrich pressed his case. Evangelical leaders, especially those whose schools were affected by the ruling, were angry, electing to construe the [court] decision as government intrusion on religious matters. Weyrich used the *Green v. Connally* case to rally evangelicals against the government. When "the Internal Revenue

---

v. Joseph R. Biden, Jr., President of the United States, et al., No. 21-2270 (8th Cir. 2022), https://tinyurl.com/52v2y8hp. Italics mine.

6. Randall Balmer, "The Real Origins of the Religious Right," *Politico*, May 27, 2014, https://tinyurl.com/2d52p7jm.

Service tried to deny tax exemption to private schools," Weyrich said in an interview with *Conservative Digest*, that "more than any single act brought the fundamentalists and evangelicals into the political process." The IRS action "kicked a sleeping dog," Richard Viguerie, one of the founders of the New Right, said. "It was the episode that ignited the religious right's involvement in real politics." When *Conservative Digest* cataloged evangelical discontent with Jimmy Carter in August 1979, the Internal Revenue Service regulations headed the list.[7]

Balmer continues, arguing that in "ramping up for political activism, evangelicals portrayed themselves as defending what they considered the sanctity of the evangelical subculture from outside influence."[8] Consider the title of the above-mentioned Christian Legal Organization in the Ozarks case, Alliance Defending Freedom (ADF).[9] This has been one of the legal entities supporting most of the major Supreme Court challenges on religious freedom, especially on behalf of evangelicals. The current Speaker of the House is a former ADF lawyer.

This notion of defending the evangelical subculture against outside threats forms the central thesis of sociologist Christian Smith's classic *American Evangelicalism: Embattled and Thriving*.[10] Smith's subtitle underscores what he calls "a subcultural identity theory of religious persistence." In this light, the evangelical subculture positions itself against the broader world, seeing itself as the remnant of true faith battling against the forces of secularism. He writes: "Amer-

7. Randall Balmer, *Bad Faith: Race and the Rise of the Religious Right* (Grand Rapids: Eerdmans, 2021), 53–54.

8. Balmer, *Bad Faith*, 54.

9. Daniel Bennett, *Defending Faith: The Politics of the Christian Conservative Legal Movement* (Lawrence: University Press of Kansas, 2017), is an excellent resource on these organizations.

10. Christian Smith, *American Evangelicalism: Embattled and Thriving* (Chicago: University of Chicago Press, 1998).

ican evangelicalism, we contend, is strong not because it is shielded against, but because it is—or at least perceives itself to be— embattled with forces that seem to oppose or threaten it. Indeed, evangelical-ism, we suggest, thrives on distinction, engagement, tension, conflict, and threat. Without these, evangelicalism would lose its identity and purpose and grow languid and aimless. Thus, we will argue, the evan-gelical movement's vitality is not a product of its protected isolation from, but of its vigorous engagement with pluralistic modernity."[11]

Smith argues that the strength of the subcultural identity of evan-gelicals is a function of the group's success in creating a "morally ori-enting collective identit[y]," positing that "those religious groups will be relatively stronger which better possess and employ the cultural tools needed to create both clear distinction from and significant en-gagement and tension with other relevant subgroups, short of becom-ing genuinely countercultural."[12]

For the evangelical subcultural identity to thrive, there needs to be not only a distinction between inside and outside views but also a perceived threat from "them." This is why a Christian university's leadership feels it necessary to sue the federal government over a rule that (1) hasn't taken effect and (2) was never intended to apply to col-lege dormitories. While the current policy initiative might in itself be relatively benign, when seen from within the subcultural framework, it presents a potential downstream risk, especially if used as a weapon against Christians.

> Finally, at the farthest extreme of cultural tension and conflict, some, but certainly not all, evangelicals see external threats even more menacing than a displaced heritage and demotion to second-class citizenship. More than a few evangelicals are concerned by what they believe are increasingly powerful, organized groups in America with clearly anti-Christian agendas. To be sure, some evangelicals express tremendous self-confidence and see no partic-

11. Smith, *American Evangelicalism*, 89.
12. Smith, *American Evangelicalism*, 119.

ular conspiracy set on undermining Christianity. However, other evangelicals do discern rumblings of what they fear could become a frightful future. And yet others, a definite minority, are convinced that the barbarians are already now battering down the gates.[13]

It's been a quarter century since Smith wrote his book. Much has changed in the world of evangelicalism over that time. One of the greatest changes is seen in the more cosmopolitan views of today's Christian university students. They are far less likely to see antagonism in the larger culture than was true of earlier cohorts. Moreover, the leaders of Christian universities—administrators, trustees, donors, denominational stakeholders—are much more likely to adopt the embattled subcultural identity than is true of the students they hope to reach and the faculty who will teach them.

Toward the end of the book, Smith argues that the attempts to fight culture wars (not his phrase) by those in the evangelical subculture not only fail to change the trends they are hoping to challenge but may backfire. At best, the evangelicals fighting battles are simply ignored as out of touch. At worst, they seriously damage the future strength of the movement: "Only a minority of nonevangelicals believe that evangelicals are offering helpful answers either to people's personal problems and moral questions or to America's social, economic, and political problems. The vast majority said either no, evangelicals are not offering good answers or that they simply do not know one way or the other. Either way is bad news for evangelicals. Evangelicals may believe in the practical moral superiority of their particular Christian way of life. But most other Americans apparently do not see it that way."[14]

Christian Smith isn't the only sociologist who has attempted to understand American evangelicalism. James Davison Hunter, mentioned in the last chapter, published a series of books between 1983 and 1991 exploring how the challenge of modernity caused evangelicals to

13. Smith, *American Evangelicalism*, 142.
14. Smith, *American Evangelicalism*, 187.

withdraw into closed systems and embrace the culture-war motif.[15] In 2010, he reflected on the dynamic relationship between cultural identity and modern pluralism and found the extant tactics lacking.[16] He writes: "The deeper irony, though, is that in the Christian faith, one has the possibility of relatively autonomous institutions and practices that could—in both judgment and affirmation—be a source of ideals and values capable of elevating politics to more than the quest for power. But the consequences of the whole-hearted and uncritical embrace of politics by Christians has been, in effect, to reduce Christian faith to a political ideology and various Christian denominations and para-church organizations to special interest groups."[17]

As both sociologists recognize, evangelical institutions, including universities, use culture-war approaches for two reasons: to demonstrate in-group solidarity and to take a stand against the broader culture. The unfortunate reality is that culture wars do not work on either front.

Internally, culture warriors in Christian higher education are required to downplay the extant level of diversity of opinion. The standard position is presented as "simple common sense" or "Christian tradition" and places dissenters in a negative light. Those dissenters, acknowledging their discomfort, may simply opt to leave. Meanwhile, as Smith noted, the culture warriors celebrating their traditionalism strike the outside world as retrograde and rightfully treated with suspicion. This, in turn, makes future recruitment and social influence more difficult, as institutions led by culture warriors are seen as primarily politically motivated, as Hunter observed.

15. James Davison Hunter, *American Evangelicalism: Conservative Religion and the Quandary of Modernity* (New Brunswick, NJ: Rutgers University Press, 1983); James Davison Hunter, *Evangelicals: The Coming Generation* (Chicago: University of Chicago Press, 1987); James Davison Hunter, *Culture Wars: The Struggle to Define America* (New York: Basic Books, 1991).

16. James Davison Hunter, *To Change the World: The Irony, Tragedy, and Possibility of Christianity in the Late Modern World* (New York: Oxford University Press, 2010).

17. Hunter, *To Change the World*, 172.

LGBTQ+ Issues in Christian Universities

Perhaps no issue offers a greater example of the limitations of an institutional culture-war approach than the question of LGBTQ+ policies.[18] In the wake of the 2015 *Obergefell* decision, two institutions in the CCCU—Goshen College and Eastern Mennonite University (EMU)—announced that they were changing their HR policy to allow the hiring of faculty and staff in same-sex marriages.[19] This change came from two sources: discussions within the Mennonite Church USA and internal demand from students and some faculty.

The Mennonite Church USA, long known for its commitments to diversity and human rights, entertained a proposal from a group called Pink Menno to change their stance on LGBTQ+ issues.[20] Instead, the Mennonites adopted what they called a "forbearance resolution."[21] The resolution stated that the denomination recognized that differences of opinion existed in the body on LGBTQ+ issues and that they should commit to remaining in community. It was after the forbearance resolution was adopted that Goshen and EMU changed their policies.

The response from other members of the CCCU community was swift, demanding the two schools be removed from membership. The CCCU president opted to gather input from the entire CCCU board.

18. The following section builds upon a conference presentation I made in 2016 at the North Central Sociological Association. John W. Hawthorne, "Crisis in the Council for Christian Colleges and Universities: A Case Study of Fragmenting Evangelical Infrastructure" (North Central Sociological Association, Chicago, IL, March 25, 2016).

19. Bob Smietana, Morgan Lee, and Sarah Eekhoff Zylstra, "Two CCCU Colleges to Allow Same-Sex Married Faculty," *Christianity Today*, July 28, 2015, https://tinyurl.com/2vyssas3.

20. "About," accessed March 21, 2016, http://www.pinkmenno.org/history-vision/.

21. Mennonite Church USA, "Forbearance in the Midst of Differences – 2015," July 2, 2015, https://tinyurl.com/yc85hnzy.

Even that proved too liberal for some members. Union University and Oklahoma Wesleyan University were the first two institutions to withdraw their membership in protest. Others followed. Eventually, Goshen and EMU also removed themselves to avoid controversy, as have other institutions.

In 2015, membership in the CCCU required potential institutions to (1) be undergraduate liberal arts institutions accredited by one of the US regional accrediting bodies; (2) have a mission statement reflecting a commitment to being a "Christ-centered institution"; (3) ensure that their faculty and staff express a personal faith in Jesus Christ; (4) be supportive of other Christian colleges and universities and have a commitment to advance the cause of Christian higher education through participation in the programs of the CCCU and payment of the annual dues; and (5) be responsible in financial and ethical matters as an institution.[22] Nothing in the membership criteria required affirmation of traditional marriage. They did, however, still suggest that members support other member institutions, which would seem to put the dissenters out of compliance with the membership criteria.

Today, the CCCU still lists the same five criteria but adds an additional section titled "Christian Distinctives and Advocacy." This new section requires that institutions affirm that God is Creator, that humans are to be treated with worth and dignity, that the gospel is one of reconciliation, and that sexual relations should be limited to marriage between one man and one woman.[23]

However, students within CCCU institutions have continued to push for a more inclusive stance. Several institutions have approved student groups that provide support for queer students and their allies (causing great consternation among some constituents). Increasingly,

22. For more on this, see Hawthorne, "Crisis in the Council for Christian Colleges and Universities: A Case Study of Fragmenting Evangelical Infrastructure."

23. Council for Colleges and Universities, "Membership Application," 2022, https://tinyurl.com/4pcs8ud7.

institutions are finding the freedom to change their policies even if it means becoming an affiliate member of the CCCU or dropping out altogether. In recent years, Belmont University, Eastern University, and Whitworth University have all changed their policies on staff and faculty in same-sex marriages.[24]

Many other institutions have found themselves caught between the views of their students and younger alumni, on the one hand, and their trustees and denominational sponsors, on the other. Both Seattle Pacific University and Calvin University have been in the crosshairs for years. The sponsoring denominations of both schools have reinforced their opposition to LGBTQ+ accommodation and threatened them with a loss of their ability to continue if they changed their policies.

I've reflected on the monumental change in attitudes that has occurred among the current generation of students about homosexuality in general and same-sex marriage in particular. To them, the HR policies and strident chapel addresses are seen as gross intolerance.

This look at LGBTQ+ issues in the CCCU provides some lessons about the limitations of the culture-war approach some Christian universities are tempted to take. As Christian Smith has argued, drawing these lines in the sand is a means of developing in-group solidarity in the face of perceived threat.[25] That sense of embattlement requires unanimity from the CCCU perspective, which is why it was important to change the membership criteria. There may be Christian schools that are more affirming, but they can no longer be in the CCCU.

24. Jonathan S. Coley, *Gay on God's Campus: Mobilizing for LGBT Equality at Christian Colleges and Universities* (Chapel Hill: University of North Carolina Press, 2018), provides an excellent case study of how Belmont University changed its policy. I say more on Belmont in chapter 7.

25. Although CCCU schools have long feared that the federal government will require them to affirm LGBTQ+ students or else lose their federal aid, the government has generally been accepting of their religious preferences. I've long argued that this fear is the result of strong ties between the CCCU and Christian legal organizations like the Alliance Defending Freedom.

Of course, in a modern social media age, drawing such harsh lines in the sand brings more opprobrium. Schools are seen as anachronistic, which makes it harder to develop good relations with prospective students, faculty, and donors.

Students and younger alumni have found ways to push back. Protests in support of LGBTQ+ students, particularly around the need for affinity groups within student development, are quite common. Alumni groups have effectively used social media to draw attention to what they see as out-of-touch administrations (which ignore them in the short term).

In summary, efforts by Christian universities to avoid addressing student, alumni, and public concerns over LGBTQ+ engagement illustrate the limits of a culture-war approach. Every attempt to bracket a controversial topic, whether sexual orientation or gender identity or racial injustice or political ideology, will create ongoing crises. On the one hand, schools will take pride in "holding the line." On the other, they will be seen as out of touch and reactionary.

Culture Making, Not Culture Wars

Earlier I wrote that James Davison Hunter had come to see the culture-war motif as lacking. If Hunter sees limited value in contemporary culture wars (as well as cultural accommodation and cultural isolation), what is the appropriate stance for a Christian university preparing students for a changing culture? How are those students to become the change agents the mission statements in chapter 2 call for if they don't learn to engage the culture?

Hunter's answer lies in what he calls "faithful presence." He explains this stance as follows:

> This, in short, is the foundation of a theology of faithful presence. It can be summarized in two essential lessons for our time. *The first is that incarnation is the only adequate reply to the challenges of dissolution; the erosion of trust between word and the world and the*

problems that attend to it. From this follows the second: *it is the way the Word became incarnate in Jesus Christ and the purposes to which the incarnation was directed that are the only adequate challenge of difference.* For the Christian, if there is a possibility for human flourishing in a world such as ours, it begins when God's word of love becomes flesh in us, is embodied in us, is enacted through us and in so doing, a trust is forged between the word spoken and the reality to which it speaks; to the words we speak and the realities to which we, the church, point. In all, presence and place matter decisively.[26]

The faithful Christian university avoids culture wars and opts instead for faithful presence. That requires a stance that sees the surrounding culture not as a hostile environment but as a place where faculty and graduates engage the broader world. And this engagement is not a matter of exercising dominion but stems from the recognition of a shared culture in which God is active. Rather than building institutional identity through culture wars, it enhances the culture through culture making.

Makoto Fujimura picks up on an earlier book of Hunter's, *Culture Wars*,[27] arguing that such battles contain "an implicit yet imperious disregard for the goal of a common life."[28] In place of animus toward "the other," a commitment to culture creation affirms the value of all parties, finding a new way forward: "Culture care starts with the identification and articulation of brokenness. It creates a safe space for truth telling. But it does not stop there. It starts with listening and then invites people onward toward beauty, wholeness, and healing. As we become able to acknowledge the truth of our situation and can

26. Hunter, *To Change the World*, 241.

27. James Davison Hunter, *Culture Wars: The Struggle to Define America* (New York: Basic Books, 1991).

28. Makoto Fujimura, *Culture Care: Reconnecting with Beauty for Our Common Life* (Downers Grove, IL: InterVarsity Press, 2017), 39.

tell that story, we are encouraged to move into caring for artists and all other participants in the culture, into creating contexts for deeper conversation, into fostering spiritual growth, and sometimes into problem solving."[29]

While Fujimura is generally speaking of the work of the artist, his insights are relevant to considering how the fearless Christian university might chart new paths within the context of contentious issues that so often create challenges. Consider this reference to the familiar Christian metaphor of sheep and shepherds:

> In recent years, many churches and communities have missed this point. We have created rigid tribal boundaries with high barriers and closed gates to keep our sheep in the pen, safe from the wider world. Ironically, closed gates mandate the extra labor and expense of bringing in stale, dry fodder—everything "Christian" needed to feed the flock—for sheep who should be grazing green pastures for themselves.
>
> *This leaves our lively young sheep with a perceived choice between complying with a community's norms and starving culturally, or leaping the fence to get cultural nourishment.* Our call as leaders and pastors is instead to open the gate and guide them to greener pastures.[30]

So how do those previously committed to culture wars find ways of opening the gate to the issues that divide us? When far too much of the plausibility structure of the Christian university has been devoted to fence building and monitoring those who get too close to the edges, can the universities manage to lean into the brokenness Fujimura describes?

The way forward is to lean into the uncertainties of the current conflicts. It involves working with those ambiguities and, through di-

---

29. Fujimura, *Culture Care*, 46.
30. Fujimura, *Culture Care*, 87. Italics mine.

alogue, creating the kinds of new cultural approaches that are needed for the Christian university, its students, its faculty, its trustees, its stakeholders, and its public.

Andy Crouch, in his book *Culture Making*, imagines exactly this kind of work (albeit not exactly with universities in mind). He argues that when culture is seen through a worldview lens, culture warriors miss the fact that "cultural goods have a life of their own."[31]

Once battle lines are drawn, it becomes nearly impossible to find new paths. But new paths are the only way forward. New paths require a willingness to create new cultural forms that aren't trapped by the former battle lines: "All culture making requires a choice, conscious or unconscious, to take our place in a cultural tradition. We cannot make culture without culture. And this means that *creation begins with cultivation*—taking care of the good things that culture has already handed on to us. The first responsibility of culture makers is not to make something new but to become fluent in the cultural traditions to which we are responsible. Before we can be culture makers, we must be culture keepers."[32]

I would suggest further that culture making instead of culture warring requires a commitment to what Walter Brueggemann calls "prophetic imagination."[33] He argues that empire (or power) has shaped too much of how the church (and, by extension, the Christian university) sees itself. The alternative to this commitment to empire thinking is to become open to the risk-taking of new perspectives. Calling the old empire thinking a "totalism," he suggests an alternative:

> The totalism imagines itself absolute to perpetuity, while the prophetic imagination—in contradiction—imagines an old world ending and a new world emerging. It is a contest of imaginations

31. Andy Crouch, *Culture Making: Recovering Our Creative Calling* (Downers Grove, IL: InterVarsity Press, 2008).

32. Crouch, *Culture Making*, 74–75.

33. Walter Brueggemann, *The Prophetic Imagination*, 40th anniversary ed. (Minneapolis: Fortress Press, 2018).

that admits no easy resolution but that puts the hearer in crisis between a failed imagination and a new inexplicable imagination. In the formation of Scripture's canon, that contest between imaginations is resolved on behalf of prophetic imagination while dismissing the imagination of the totalism. Prophetic imagination is judged in this canon to be adequately truthful, even when on occasion historical events say otherwise.[34]

Culture making requires a stance of partnership with the broader culture rather than the previous oppositional identity. This shift transforms the Christian university from a place cut off from the culture to one that is working alongside it for mutual benefit. Hunter describes how such a shift means that the Christian university must change the terms that frame its vision and approach:

> I have argued throughout this treatise that we need a new language for how the church engages the culture. It is essential, in my view, to abandon altogether talk of "redeeming the culture," "advancing the kingdom," and "changing the world." Christians need to leave such language behind them because it carries too much weight. It implies conquest, take-over, or dominion, which in my view is precisely what God does not call us to pursue—at least not in any conventional, twentieth- or twenty-first-century way of understanding those terms.[35]

What might this paradigmatic shift mean for institutions of Christian higher education? What might these abstract shifts suggest for life in the Christian university?

As a start, it's important to acknowledge the unique set of factors contributing to the Christian university's ability to transition to a culture-making model. First, Christian universities attract a host of interested students who are trying to define their place in a rapidly

34. Brueggemann, *Prophetic Imagination*, 130.
35. Hunter, *To Change the World*, 280.

changing world. Second, they have faculty and student-development staff who share similar faith commitments and therefore can provide a safe space to explore challenging conversations. Third, elements of university life such as chapels, small groups, lecture series, and the like make such work feasible. Fourth, faculty can bring the best scholarship from their disciplines to bear on this matter. Fifth, a significant number of students are looking to enter ministry roles, whether in professional or volunteer roles. Their work of culture creation rather than culture wars will have a long-term impact on the congregations they serve. Sixth, younger alumni experiencing the world after graduation want to know that the Christian university is addressing important issues and preparing incoming cohorts for life after graduation. The failure to address these issues has limited younger alumni giving, even considering their meager financial resources in the first years after college. Finally, many Christian universities serve as reference points and professional-development sites for pastors and churches in their region or denomination.

Were these factors aligned under a culture-making model, working in harmony to address the complexities of pressing social issues, the potential to develop new approaches and conversations not based in conflict might be uncovered. Instead of the recurring tensions between students and churches, alumni and administration, and ministers and faculty that come with a culture-war mindset and often lead to no-win confrontations, trust between university stakeholders might reemerge. Whereas a culture-war stance feeds the perception that the Christian university is out of touch at best and interested in discrimination at worst, a firm commitment to culture making could draw positive attention to the institution and potentially ameliorate enrollment challenges over the long run.

Using a Prophetic Imagination

It's possible to sketch some hypotheticals of how current controversial topics could be better served through a culture-making approach. I imagine that a commitment to culture making at a Christian university would result in white papers, workshops for churches, books, web pages, podcasts, and video productions. These would be seen not as niche projects of those with special interests but as institution-wide operations.

At the beginning of *The Prophetic Imagination*, Brueggemann lays out his vision for the book. It's helpful to use this vision as a frame for thinking about what culture making could look like at the Christian university: "The task of prophetic ministry is to nurture, nourish, and evoke a consciousness and perception alternative to the consciousness and perception of the dominant culture around us."[36]

That alternative consciousness stands in contrast to not only the dominant culture but also Christian-worldview culture. With that in mind, I will paint a picture of what it might look like to address three contemporary issues: structural racism, sexual harassment, and LGBTQ+ issues.

To their credit, many Christian universities have made a commitment to diversity over recent decades. While still predominantly white institutions (reflecting the demographics of evangelicalism at large), they not only increased admissions outreach but committed to intercultural offices and diversity officers. However, outside of Black History Month posters in the cafeteria each February, it hasn't fundamentally changed the culture of the institution.

When a racially insensitive incident occurs, the administration holds open forums and tries to find the best way to address concerns. Yet once the current incident has passed, institutional culture reverts to the norm.

A more forceful systemic response opens the door to accusations of supporting critical race theory that we saw in the Grove City College case. Imagine, instead of the open forums mentioned above, a series of campus conversations around race. Perhaps older alumni could be asked to reflect on the white dominance when they went to the college. Older representatives from predominantly Black churches

36. Brueggemann, *Prophetic Imagination*, 3.

that have sent students to the university could tell their Jim Crow stories. Younger representatives from the university and the churches could speak about their current experience. The conversations might culminate in a multiday celebration of the institution's history, a service of institutional repentance for policies and inaction that compounded structural racism,[37] and an enhanced sense of partnership with the Black community that has enriched the university. The celebration could occur on campus and at affiliated churches, including Black churches.

The issue of sexual harassment is a challenging one for Christian universities. On the one hand, parents have hopes that while at college their children will meet and marry someone who shares their faith. Celebrations of student and alumni engagements are common (even though the gender imbalance at most schools means that most will not have the experience).

Christian universities have developed policies defining sexual harassment and the processes by which they will be investigated. But as both the #MeToo and #ChurchToo movements have shown us, having a policy is insufficient if the campus atmosphere makes reporting sexual harassment difficult.[38]

Christian universities have clear policies forbidding premarital sex and outlining sanctions for violations.[39] Yet the pressure from parents and others for students to find a suitable Christian mate and the normative celebration of young heterosexual relationships embedded in

37. Daniel Silliman and Kate Shellnutt, "Wheaton College Releases Report on Its History of Racism," *Christianity Today*, September 14, 2023, https://tinyurl.com/frvwe755.

38. Hannah Dreyfus, "'The Liberty Way': How Liberty University Discourages and Dismisses Students' Reports of Sexual Assaults," *ProPublica*, October 14, 2021, https://tinyurl.com/yj2dw43w.

39. Although schools will take stances banning same-sex romantic behaviors (see Kathryn Post, "BYU Officially Restores Honor Code Ban on 'Same-Sex Romantic Behavior,'" Religion News Service, August 30, 2023, https://tinyurl.com/yck8dnem), it's remarkably rare for a school to limit heterosexual romantic behaviors.

the institutional culture opens the door to various forms of sexual harassment, assault, and potential date rape.

A Christian university committed to imagining new cultural possibilities might see here an opportunity for campus-wide dialogues about gender expectations, toxic masculinity, and interpersonal power. These dialogues could draw from some excellent Christian authors, female faculty and staff (with some males on the periphery), community activists, and young alumni.[40] The end product of such dialogues might be a document that underscored the commitments made to those of the opposite sex. This document would become part of the institution's orientation process and marketing materials. The university would still have a sexual harassment policy but any need to invoke it would be seen as a matter of institutional failure.

The LGBTQ+ conversation cannot be resolved with a simple campus dialogue. Those have happened in institutions across the country. Debate remains on whether the Christian university campus can be a safe place for queer students.

Some institutions have allowed gay-straight alliance or affinity groups. Others have banned such activities.

What we do know is that there are queer students at all Christian universities. Given the remarkable changes in attitudes toward same-sex relationships among young evangelicals in recent years, much of the student body believes that queer students have a right to be there. More significantly, those queer students haven't left their Christian faith behind. That's why they're at a Christian university in the first place.

And yet, many campuses are limited by their denominational sponsorship, especially when the denomination has elevated support of "traditional marriage" to doctrinal status. Because denominations own university property (and maybe the charter to operate), univer-

---

40. I once reached out to some recent female graduates to ask them what they wish they had learned at college. Several said they wish someone had told them about the likelihood of getting hit on at bars and restaurants by random males.

sities have limited room to maneuver.[41] Nondenominational schools are not bound by such constraints, so the only thing keeping them from significant engagement on the topic is the will to act.

Despite these constraints, there is still a great deal of cultural re-imagining that Christian universities can do around LGBTQ+ questions. First and foremost would be public statements by institutions that Christians hold differing views on the topic.[42] As many mainline denominations have demonstrated (some better than others), differences of interpretation on certain matters can and do exist even amid general consensus on fundamental doctrinal questions.

Additionally, Christian universities should develop clearly stated nondiscrimination policies. Campus members taking hostile action or speaking against LGBTQ+ students should face disciplinary actions. Otherwise, queer students are not full members of the community. Similarly, chapel addresses and public lectures should acknowledge the legitimate presence of the queer members of the community.

These adjustments would make clear that queer students belong as true members of the community (as many colleges have claimed in principle). There is no need to draw lines around their interpersonal behaviors, since there are already limits on premarital sex. Is it possible that the campus would have to see two members of the same sex holding hands crossing campus? Yes. But unless the school is willing to ban all public displays of affection (which many would welcome), this is only fair.

In short, there is a host of cultural artifacts that can be developed supporting queer students that do not require the Christian university to declare itself affirming. For institutions that pride themselves on embracing Christian community, this is a minimum accommodation.

---

41. I'll return to this challenge in chapter 8.

42. Fuller Seminary was considering this wording in spring 2024. See Deepa Bharath, "California Evangelical Seminary Ponders Changes That Would Make It More Welcoming to LGBTQ Students," AP News, https://tinyurl.com/383mjn2v.

It is fear that keeps Christian universities from taking these steps in culture making. The fear of public scorn feeds culture wars. The fear of losing one's way keeps institutions from developing prophetic imagination in tune with a changing world. It doesn't have to be this way. Institutions swapping culture wars for faithful presence expressed in creative, culture-making ways have the potential not only to stay true to their historic academic mission but to do so with confidence.

CHAPTER FIVE

Faculty and Administration in Partnership

If an institution is to achieve the status of being a fearless Christian university, a fruitful partnership between its administrators and faculty must be built. For far too much of recent history, the administrative and faculty roles have been in opposition.[1]

This is not unique to Christian universities, of course. The tensions between administrators and faculty are understandable considering several sociological factors. First, while the faculty in their teaching roles are focused on the internal dynamics of the institution, the administration is outwardly focused on branding, reputation, donors, and churches. Second, faculty members largely view themselves through their disciplinary identity, while administrators are more likely to see them as operational units to be managed. Third, increasingly college presidents are drawn from ranks outside the classroom. Trustee search committees look for transformational leaders who will innovate and build new models of financial sustainability, skills which can turn faculty into obstacles to be overcome.

These factors combine to create the challenges in Christian universities so often reported in *Inside Higher Ed* or the *Chronicle of Higher Education*. How did faculty take a vote of no-confidence on an in-

---

1. Senior leaders in student development are something of an anomaly here. Though part of university administration, their proximity to students and focus on student well-being leaves them with sympathies and perspectives closer to those of faculty.

coming president even before he was inaugurated? Why did academic leaders suddenly fire English professors because they used Jemar Tisby's book (or even just a quote from it) in their syllabi? Why is tenure under threat? Why was the 1941 American Association of University Professors academic freedom statement redefined to protect the institution first and the faculty member second? Are professors at Christian universities truly free to pursue their teaching and scholarship, or are they considered ministers first?

The answers to these varied questions all speak to a failure to understand the central role of the university. In *The Real World of College*, Fischman and Gardner argue that alignment among constituent parts is key to pursuing institutional mission.[2] In the fearless Christian university, that alignment centers on the building of a robust academic community. The Christian university is not simply about friendships, small size, sports, and chapel. Rather, the academic experiences of faculty, students, and even administrators are the core of their shared activity.

If the fearless Christian university is to pursue the initiatives suggested throughout this book, a more functional partnership between faculty and administrators is required. Such a partnership requires consistent interaction between faculty and administrators, not simply in meetings and other formal settings but around issues of social and academic significance. The academic scholarship of the faculty, appropriately supported and celebrated, should aid in the development of a sense of shared academic life. While not all scholarship would fit the culture-making model, as much as possible should.

A biology or chemistry scholar can aid the community in its understanding of issues like pandemics or global warming. Psychology and education faculty can address topics surrounding the autism scale and student mental health. Business and economics faculty can speak to issues involving institutional finance or the consumer decisions of parents. English and religion faculty can address the core meta-

2. Wendy Fischman and Howard Gardner, *The Real World of College: What Higher Education Is and What It Can Be* (Cambridge, MA: MIT Press, 2022).

phors that enhance or dissolve community. Sociologists and historians can speak to issues that feed culture wars and explore alternatives in response.

This activity happens now, but often outside the classroom. It's not uncommon for such topics to be explored in an evening lecture to a hundred or so interested students. After a good discussion (too often without any administrators present), everyone moves on to the next thing.

These somewhat peripheral activities must move to the center of the life of the fearless Christian university. Venues such as opening orientation, commencement, chapel, and homecoming would provide opportunities for celebrating shared academic commitments.

This shift from periphery to core has some major implications. Not only does it create potential partnerships between faculty and administrators, but it provides administrators with tools to address concerns that may arise among external stakeholders. The faculty scholar becomes a representative figure to be defended rather than a challenge to be addressed.

In short, a robust and trusting partnership between faculty and administrators enables the fearless Christian university to speak into the key issues of the day alongside the rest of higher education. The strength of a missionally aligned community makes that voice sustainable and meaningful to alumni for years to come.

I want to do several things in this chapter. First, I will explore three misleading analogies that hamper administration, trustee, and faculty partnership. Second, I examine the worlds of university presidents, trustees, and faculty to explore why the alignment described by Fischman and Gardner is so hard to attain. Third, I want to offer specific suggestions for how institutional alignment can be enhanced.

MISLEADING ANALOGIES AND THEIR CONSEQUENCES

Looking at Christian higher education writ large, there have been efforts to manage tensions, but they have not worked. Far too often, the separation between administrators and trustees, on the one hand, and faculty and students, on the other, have fallen into a top-down system of managing outliers. Maintenance of control is central to these efforts at managing faculty. As we will see, most trustees and cabinet officers don't have a background in academics. This makes them see faculty as a political block to be managed at best and a group to be overridden at worst.

Part of the challenge arises from a series of misleading analogies about the nature of the Christian liberal arts university. One of the most significant of these is that of seeing the university as something like a *church*. In this analogy, the president is like the pastor, the trustees are like elders, the faculty and staff are like church members, and students are like short-term attenders.

Given the preponderance of ministers and the common requirement to have committed Christians on the board of trustees, the invocation of this analogy is not surprising. It's not uncommon to have the president see himself as a minister to the community. In this analogy, that institutions would make decisions with little employee input, relying instead on what they believe is best for the institution (or perhaps even God's preferences), seems reasonable. Operating from this perspective drew institutions like Cedarville University and Bryan College to rewrite their doctrinal statements and require faculty to sign annually or leave.[3]

A second key analogy inhibiting full partnership between administration, trustees, and faculty is that of the university as *factory*. In this analogy, the university produces graduates of character who will shape the future society. We saw earlier that this was the most common phrase in mission statements.

---

3. Colleen Flaherty, "Too Small a Box? At Bryan College, Whose Name Honors a Famous Foe of Teaching Evolution, Faculty and Students Object to Being Required to Assert the Historicity of Adam and Eve," *Inside Higher Ed*, March 5, 2014, https://tinyurl.com/5d5p7wn5; Darlene Parsons, "The Justice Collective Documents Allegations That Cedarville University Violated the Higher Learning Commission Mandates," *The Wartburg Watch* (blog), April 27, 2020, https://tinyurl.com/yv4dcuww.

Taking the analogy further, the administration becomes management, and trustees the shareholders. Faculty members are the means of production, taking students from their initial state as freshmen and helping to turn them into the desired image of Christian university graduates. Faculty members' key responsibility is to teach their classes (and maybe do a little writing on the side).

Maintaining the quality of the means of production is done by ongoing scrutiny of faculty to make sure they don't vary from the desired qualities. In this light, one can understand how Gordon College tried to argue that a faculty member should be considered a minister and thereby not able to take action under human resources law.[4] The case was appealed all the way to the US Supreme Court, which declined to take up the case.

The third misleading analogy operating in Christian universities is that of the university as a *store*. Here, the trustees are the owners, and the administrators the managers. The faculty become salesclerks, providing the students (customers) with what they desire. Probably every faculty member has heard a frustrated student claim, "But I pay your salary!" Of course, student tuition falls well short of covering the cost of instruction.

The customer-is-always-right mentality that comes with the store analogy makes administrators very quick to respond to complaints and even the fear of complaints. In my years as department chair and chief academic officer, I often stood between the president and an individual faculty member or department. The president had been contacted by a parent or the pastor of a parent complaining about a particular instructor. Because somebody had complained (especially if they were an "important" somebody), there was an assumption that action should be taken. I usually tried to gather more information about what actually happened, followed up with the department chair, and mostly tried to defuse the situation. But not all academic leaders take this approach.

4. Daniel Silliman, "Gordon College Settles with Professor It Said Was a Minister," *Christianity Today*, December 16, 2022, https://tinyurl.com/25s9kfeu.

Such a mentality helps explain what causes faculty members to lose their jobs for introducing race as a central theme in a writing class.[5] It encourages institutions to take steps to limit flyers outside faculty offices or pronouns in email signatures.[6] In these latter cases, the administration might deny having any particular purpose of limiting LGBTQ+ advocacy, claiming that a generic policy "just happened" in the aftermath of concerns. Fear of the complaint is what causes a gay faculty member to stay in the closet for years, telling only a few trusted friends.[7] It is what caused Wheaton College to take such draconian action against political science professor Larycia Hawkins for sharing a picture of herself in a hijab on Facebook and saying that Muslims and Christians worshiped the same God.[8]

In all three of these analogies, faculty members are relatively powerless over institutional affairs, save the admittedly extraordinary freedom over what happens daily in the classroom. They receive little informa-

5. Helen Huiskes, "In the Fight over 'Wokeness,' Christian Colleges Feel Pressed to Pick a Side," *Chronicle of Higher Education*, August 31, 2023, https://tinyurl.com/ycyzkvuy; Jamiel Lynch and Andy Rose, "English Professor in Florida Says University Terminated His Contract after a Complaint over His Racial Justice Unit," CNN, March 16, 2023, https://tinyurl.com/2y bhda49; Bob Smietana, "Taylor Professor Julie Moore Cited Jemar Tisby on Her Syllabus. Then She Lost Her Job," Religion News Service, May 3, 2023, https://tinyurl.com/4xwwdcxb.

6. Kathryn Post, "Seattle Pacific University Targets LGBTQ Displays with New Policy, Say Critics," Religion News Service, September 29, 2023, https://tinyurl.com/y9fs8j2n; Megan Zahneis, "They Put Their Pronouns in Their Email Signatures. Then the University Dismissed Them," *Chronicle of Higher Education*, April 26, 2023, https://tinyurl.com/yc6md92z; Kathryn Post, "Wheaton College Restricts Employees' Ability to State Preferred Pronouns," Religion News Service, January 11, 2024, https://tinyurl.com/42unn59m.

7. Emma Green, "The Hidden Life of a Christian-College Professor," *New Yorker*, June 30, 2022, https://tinyurl.com/4etwbjme.

8. Ruth Graham, "What Really Caused an Evangelical College to Suspend a Professor?," *Atlantic*, December 17, 2015, https://tinyurl.com/3tsjkn2d.

tion, and what they do receive almost always includes glowing reports about next year's enrollment and budgetary strength. When the next year rolls around, they learn in an early faculty meeting that the numbers didn't materialize and benefits will be reduced. They are introduced to new structures and new administrative hires, with very limited input, if any. They are told that the trustees have mandated new programs or delivery mechanisms (as if the administration was not involved).

What options, then, are available to Christian university faculty? One is to use faculty meetings to raise concerns, but those are not structured for that kind of accountability. They could complain to the local press, but that usually ends in responses from a university communications officer and the isolation of the whistleblowing faculty member. They could file a complaint with their accrediting body, but it is very rare for those entities to involve themselves in internal disputes.

The one option that remains is a vote of no-confidence in the president, the administration, the board, or some combination thereof. Since 2021, CCCU institutions have seen no-confidence votes at Seattle Pacific, North Park, Cornerstone, and Hardin-Simmons.[9]

A no-confidence vote can be seen as a cry for help from faculty. But it is typically seen as insubordination by administrators and trustees. Unless the trustees were already looking for reasons to replace the president, they are most likely to double-down on their support for the administration in the face of faculty insurrection. The no-confidence vote will simply justify their preexisting belief that faculty members are troublemakers to be controlled.

---

9. Elise Takahama, "Seattle Pacific University Faculty Votes 'No Confidence' in Leadership after Board Upholds Discriminatory Hiring Policy," *Seattle Times*, April 21, 2021, https://tinyurl.com/49dxbjn7; Colleen Flaherty, "North Park Faculty Votes No Confidence in President," *Inside Higher Ed*, October 14, 2021, https://tinyurl.com/mrx3ks67; Scott Jaschik, "No-Confidence Vote at Cornerstone, Prior to Inauguration," *Inside Higher Ed*, October 24, 2021, https://tinyurl.com/2nzcbvd8; Mark Wingfield, "Hardin-Simmons Faculty Overwhelmingly Vote No Confidence in President," *Baptist News Global*, October 27, 2022, https://tinyurl.com/48c27bmh.

All the above factors keep the Christian university in its fearful status quo. A new way of conceiving the relationships between the various segments of university life is necessary if the institution is to become fearless and pursue its academic mission.

DIFFERING WORLDS

Given the pathways that presidents, trustees, and faculty follow to their respective roles, it is not surprising that they approach their work from unique and often divergent perspectives. Let's begin with presidents.

Presidents

In the fall of 2023, I researched the backgrounds of 130 presidents of CCCU institutions. I was interested, first, in the position they held immediately prior to taking the presidency.[10] Second, given the role that contemporary events have played in my argument, I wanted to get a rough estimate of their age.[11] Finally, I wanted to know approximately how long they had been in the role.

Nineteen (15 percent) of the presidents had come to the institution from the same role at another university. Twenty-five (19 percent) came from outside higher education altogether. This group included political or governmental leaders, nonprofit leaders, and ministry leaders. Twenty-three (18 percent) came directly out of institutional advancement. Twenty-four (18 percent) had previously held nonacademic administrative roles.[12]

The remainder of presidents had come out of academic affairs. Most of these were provosts or vice presidents of academic affairs,

---

10. This group included some interim presidents, but these often become permanent.

11. If a biography did not mention age, I used the college graduation year and assumed an age of twenty-two at that time.

12. The list included roles in finance, student life, spiritual life, enrollment, operations, and continuing education and as chief of staff.

but there were some school deans or leaders of think tanks. On the one hand, this category is the largest, at thirty-nine presidents (30 percent).

On the other hand, this means that seven in ten Christian university presidents have little recent professional experience in academic life. Having spent seventeen years as a cabinet officer, I know that my nonacademic colleagues tried to imagine their way into the faculty role but rarely succeeded. They liked faculty members individually but did not truly understand how faculty decisions were reached—only that they took longer to reach them than they wished.

If the central task of a fearless Christian university is to promote an academic experience that speaks to the key questions students bring and prepares them for their future, not just in a job but in a meaningful calling that encompasses work and faith, having a university president with limited understanding of academic life will make that task exceedingly difficult. To be fair, this is not a new reality. Decades have passed since most presidents came from the academic ranks. When institutional vision, reputation, and fundraising become the priorities of the role, a different skill set may seem fitting.

In the absence of a robust partnership with faculty, however, the messages that are central to that vision casting, reputation building, and fundraising run the risk of becoming generic statements about the value of Christian higher education rather than informed articulations of the institution's unique role and potential. In the worst version of this tendency, culture-war antagonism becomes a substitute for clearly communicating institutional mission.

Christian universities who might be open to becoming more fearless miss out on the opportunity to explain their mission and how it differs from other Christian institutions. This hampers marketing and public relations and puts them at the mercy of the kinds of attacks we saw at Grove City in chapter 1.

The median age of the 130 presidents is fifty-eight. However, it is more helpful to look at the presidents by generation. By this measure, only three are millennials (2 percent). Sixty-nine are Gen X (53 percent), fifty-seven (44 percent) are boomers, and one was born in the last year of the silent generation (less than 1 percent).

While there is certainly individual variation within generational categories, looking at the age of the Christian university presidents tells us a great deal about how well they might understand the lived experience of today's college students. If we combine the three millennial presidents with the youngest group in Gen X (i.e., those fifty and under), we get a total of twenty-eight presidents closest in age to the students (22 percent of the total). This youngest set of presidents may likely have children of junior high or high school age, giving them a better connection to the issues of most concern to the incoming class.

This is not to say that the other 102 presidents are not capable of understanding their students. But it does underscore that their Christian college experience as undergraduates has increasingly less in common with current students each year. It is likely that student concerns will be treated as something to be ignored as opposed to being understood and addressed.

A similar divide emerges when we examine how long the presidents have been in their current position. Over half (sixty-six) of the presidents are in the first five years of their tenure (although ten came from previous presidencies). Another twenty-nine are in years six through ten. Sixteen have served between eleven and fifteen years. The remaining nineteen have been in their role from sixteen to thirty-two years.

Again, while individuals may differ greatly, it's reasonable to assume that the longer a president has served in the role, the more likely he or she will be following an established pattern of leadership. Having developed a management system, it is relatively easy to keep it going. New students and faculty simply take the place of ones that have moved on.

On the other hand, there is great hope in the sixty-six presidents who are new to the role. Not only might they be closer in age to the current students, but they have not yet settled into a pattern of administration. This suggests that they may be the most likely group to engage in the kind of reorientation I'm calling for in this book.

Trustees

Of course, presidents cannot operate entirely on their own. Trustees of the institution have as their primary responsibility the hiring, evaluation, and continuation of the president. I analyzed some trustee backgrounds using a sample of five schools (130 would be daunting!). The size of the board of trustees was similar across the five. Four had between twenty-one and twenty-five members. The fifth had thirty-four.

Trustees are selected because they can connect to resources, think strategically, provide financial oversight, or represent specific institutional constituencies. According to the Association of Governing Boards of Universities and Colleges, *"Each board member must rise to the challenge of aligning their work with the governing board and administration in order to best serve their institution's mission. AGB empowers all board members to become highly effective trustees who fulfill their fiduciary duties and govern with confidence."*[13] This is the goal whether trustees are at Christian universities or not. Focusing on all aspects of the institutional mission within the context of sound financial oversight is key.

My analysis of trustee backgrounds at these five Christian universities found that the largest category, 30 percent, came from business, finance, or investment occupations. The second most common, 28 percent, came from ministry (either pastors or parachurch work). Nonprofits, government, and the law accounted for 16 percent, and science, technology, and medicine, 16 percent. Trustees coming from K–12 education or higher education accounted for 8 percent, and 2 percent were from the arts.

13. "Board Member," Roles & Responsibilities, Association of Governing Boards of Universities and Colleges, accessed April 20, 2024, https://tinyurl.com/nxnpmt6r. Italics added.

As with most university presidents and presidential cabinets, trustees approach their task from the periphery of the academic experience. This does not mean that they don't care about academic issues but only that they are not well versed in academic culture and too often fall back on what they know from their daily work experience. At best, they are alumni drawing from the memories of their own time as undergraduates.

An in-depth interview with a longtime Christian university trustee helped flesh out these challenges.[14] Unlike most of his trustee colleagues, he had served the university in a variety of roles, including as an adjunct faculty member while serving as trustee. He is, I told him, something of a unicorn in higher education, having the background and trust to directly engage the president and trustees on important issues. He told me that it was key for trustees to engage in "generative leadership," always moving the institution forward by developing future leaders. He contrasted that with the sentiment of far too many trustees, who seem to think their role is to support the president (and administration) regardless of the potential fallout.

Faculty

For faculty, I wanted to follow a similar pattern to the analysis of trustees, so I selected five Christian universities whose academic catalogs listed the educational background of faculty. These five schools—with a total of 473 full-time faculty members—reflect different parts of the country. I was particularly interested in what percentage of the faculty earned their bachelor's degrees at Christian universities and what percentage were alumni.[15]

Taken together, 49 percent of faculty at these five schools had completed their undergraduate studies at a CCCU school, and 25 percent were alumni of the institutions they now serve. It is quite likely that

14. Ray Rood, interview with the author, December 15, 2023.
15. I didn't count small Lutheran or Catholic schools even though the academic ethos would be similar.

the faculty members are teaching at these schools precisely because of the quality of their own undergraduate experience. Even if they had frustrations at times with their alma mater, they came back to make a difference.

This suggests that, broadly speaking, faculty members may have a clearer sense of the values of the institution than trustees and administrators do. This is true in terms of not just academic life but the entirety of the Christian university experience. Furthermore, they have had front row seats to the shifts in student outlook over the years, which has required them to accommodate perspectives they might not have held or even encountered as undergraduates.

Despite the institutional expertise afforded by their role, faculty members have too often been seen as disinterested at best and obstacles at worst. Some of this is part of an industry-wide shift in higher education toward top-down management, which threatens academic freedom, tenure, and shared governance. A broader climate of suspicion, encouraged by conservative politicians attacking universities and endless media pieces asking whether college is worth it, has likewise put faculty on the defensive.

Such attitudes are problematic throughout all of higher education, but their presence in institutions that claim to be Christian is especially troubling—and dangerous.

A BETTER ANALOGY

For Christian universities to thrive, the misleading analogies discussed above need to be replaced. A fearless Christian university must overcome the natural division among its stakeholders and promote dialogue among them. A promising path forward, I would propose, is to reenvision the Christian university as a *laboratory* that explores contemporary issues within the context of its diverse faith commitments. Living into the laboratory analogy will require significant change from presidents, trustees, and faculty. Engaging students in this work is also important, and therefore they are the focus of the next two chapters.

It is important for presidents to legitimize these laboratory dialogues by making clear to stakeholders that culture making is central to the university's mission. It is equally important for the president to engage the dialogue with an open mind and from the standpoint of a participant rather than a gatekeeper.

As I thought about these proposed changes in focus, I remembered a trip I made in 2002 to Whitworth University. I had met Bill Robinson, Whitworth's president at the time, at another school's presidential inauguration. After receiving a copy of his book, *Leading People from the Middle*,[16] I asked if I could come to Spokane and shadow him for a couple of days.

It was a wonderful time, and I saw him putting the ideas from the book into practice (even though he was already telling me what more he wished he'd included). The idea of "leading from the middle" was that there is much about leadership that involves understanding those being led. In fact, they are more partners than passive followers.

One part of the book contrasts four leadership styles: authoritarian, democratic, task-oriented, and relationship-oriented. While different presidents no doubt have differing styles, the value of the relationship piece, combined with either task orientation or a broadly democratic form of leadership, was particularly effective.

In my experience, it is the relationship piece that presidents need to work on most. This can be something as simple as regularly joining faculty members for lunch or popping into someone's office to hear what is bringing them joy. This is especially true for the 70 percent of presidents who don't immediately come from an academic background. The more they understand faculty motivations, attitudes, and fears, the better they can build consensus on how to address the big issues confronting the university.

A related issue arises out of the task-oriented leadership style. Presidents and the members of their cabinet must be problem solvers. It's

16. William P. Robinson, *Leading People from the Middle: The Universal Mission of Heart and Mind* (Provo, UT: Executive Excellence Publishing, 2002). Following his retirement, Robinson served as interim president of the CCCU.

one of the central parts of the job description to identify existing or potential problems and determine how to address them.

There is a lesson here that I learned far too late in my administrative career: sharing the nature of a problem widely when first noticed, to allow all stakeholders time to find potential solutions, is key to bringing people along. Maybe administrators are simply protective as a rule, but I have seen far too many express concern in a cabinet meeting while publicly putting forth a happy face to keep morale up. While waiting for news from the administration, faculty tend to worry that nobody's minding the store. I pointed out to all presidents I served that in the absence of information, faculty tend to invent the worst possible version of events. When the solution finally is announced, it is too often shared as "it could have been worse."

By building relationships with faculty (especially, but not exclusively, tenured faculty), presidents develop the trust to lead the institution into unchartered waters. This is not to say that all faculty will agree with every such move, but there would be a reservoir of trust undergirding the discussions.

Trustees can embrace the laboratory analogy as well, but this too will require a shift in orientation. The board is only on campus a few times a year for a couple of days at a time. Their primary charge is the hiring and evaluation of the president. Beyond that, they are to ensure financial stability and look out for the institution's mission and vision.

It is not surprising, given trustee backgrounds, that their comfort level is highest with what they know from their world outside the university. Normally, this means a focus on finances, marketing, and recruiting. In terms of mission, as we saw earlier, trustees may be most likely to try to sustain the institution's mission as they saw it expressed when they were undergraduates.

If trustees are to serve a fearless Christian university, the concern over mission cannot be backward-looking and nostalgic. The central task is to foresee the implications of the university's mission twenty years into the future and how institutional ethos is maintained within a changing social environment.

Trustees need far more training in how to go about conducting this analysis. It is insufficient to give them an endless diet of demographic-cliff warnings, stories about college costs, and concerns about real or potential lawsuits. Open conversations can take place only if partnerships with administration and faculty have been established.

Far too many universities have formal and informal barriers separating trustees from faculty members. This, in part, reflects earlier periods where faculty members would take standard administrative complaints to individual trustee members. It is also a reflection of the backgrounds of the trustees; not understanding academics well, they are not particularly interested in the lives of faculty.

Some institutions allow a faculty representative to sit in on trustee meetings. Perhaps they are invited to give a statement to the academic affairs committee. But generally, their role is to represent the faculty and report back on what happened in the meeting.

Moving toward a fearless future will require far more interaction between trustees and faculty.[17] This goes beyond a periodic reception or dinner. It likely means inviting some faculty members to board retreats. The two groups need enough of a relationship to be able to speak freely and think creatively together in a safe environment.

Naturally, certain safeguards would be necessary. Such interactions would not be venues for criticisms of the administration or sorting out personnel disputes. But laying a groundwork of trust and finding a safe place to address difficult questions confronting the university is crucial.

Moving toward the sense of partnership I'm outlining will require a lot from the faculty as well. A first step for most faculty members would be a shift from a disciplinary orientation to an institutional orientation. This doesn't mean that sociology professors will stop being sociology professors or that theology professors will stop being theology professors. It does mean that in the grand scheme of things, their interests lie in seeing the institution, and not simply their own

---

17. I discuss this in depth in chapter 9.

careers, thrive over time. This might be more of a shift for senior faculty than those early in their career.

Brian Rosenberg, former president of Macalester College, has argued that faculty members "are less like a baseball team and more like an all-star team."[18] Shifting to an institutional orientation will require faculty to see themselves as role players rather than all-stars. Some members of the faculty—for example, those focused on preparing students for careers—might not play a larger institutional role. However, faculty members who embrace an institutional orientation with an eye toward the future can play a key role in helping administrators and trustees navigate difficult waters. This is much more likely to involve public scholarship than peer-reviewed disciplinary work and must be acknowledged and affirmed by promotion and tenure committees. Frankly, it could be argued that the Christian university benefits more from such public scholarship than from the best scholarly publication in the top disciplinary journal.

Faculty members who like to boast of "speaking truth to power" could actually bring about change. Difficult questions could be articulated, and a range of options considered. And because these roles would be authorized by the institution, the faculty would be protected from accusations of disloyalty from external parties who think that these difficult questions should not be discussed.

This is no doubt a lot to ask. Many institutions may not have the internal dynamics to attempt the shifts I've described here. But I'd argue that not all institutions have to follow this path—just some. Part of what holds Christian universities back is that they all seem to be afraid of being the first one to chart a new path.

The competition along the current path is going to get even more intense in the coming decade. Not every school can follow the model of a Cedarville or a Liberty. Someone must provide the proof of the concept that a fearless way is possible.

18. Brian Rosenberg, *"Whatever It Is, I'm Against It": Resistance to Change in Higher Education* (Cambridge, MA: Harvard Education Press, 2023), 86.

AN ILLUSTRATION THAT ALMOST WORKED

After the above-mentioned vote of no-confidence in the board of trustees at Seattle Pacific University (SPU), the trustees brought in a consultant to help them figure out next steps. It is to their credit that they took this step rather than strike back against those who pushed the no-confidence vote. The consultant, a former Christian university president, helped them develop a process involving a work group made up of trustees, faculty, and administrators.[19]

The central question was how SPU could respond to requests from students, faculty, and alumni that its policy against hiring LGBTQ+ faculty and staff be changed. Could SPU make such a change and retain its Christian identity? What would it mean for a self-identified ecumenical community affiliated with the Free Methodist Church to wrestle with being a hospitable community?

The work group was made up of four trustees, four faculty members, and several administrators (including the interim president). The group met at least every two weeks for a year. They developed a series of potential options, one of which was to leave the current policy in place.

As this received little support from the group, they developed what they called the "Third Way."[20] This path acknowledged SPU's broad sense of ecumenicism on a variety of fronts rather than seeing it solely as a Free Methodist institution.

One stipulation of the work group was that any recommendations had to be kept confidential until they could be presented to the full board of trustees. The trustee cochair would present the options and the faculty cochair would make recommendations.

However, prior to the process reaching its conclusion, a board member who was a leader in the Free Methodist Church informed

19. Material for this section taken from interviews by the author with work-group cochairs Joshua Canada (December 1, 2023) and Kevin Neuhouser (November 3, 2023).

20. "SPU LGBTQIA+ Timeline," SPU Faculty Action, accessed April 20, 2024, https://tinyurl.com/yc3xkw2w.

denominational leaders what was under consideration. That trustee shared a white paper with the denomination that the work groups never saw. The denominational leadership changed the official church policy regarding LGBTQ+ and traditional marriage, which removed the option that was under discussion.

The move seriously damaged the mutual trust the faculty and board had been working to build. It left the faculty with little option but to raise concerns with SPU's accrediting body, a real step backward from what was initially envisioned.

Seattle Pacific's process nevertheless shows what might be possible when a Christian university is free to operate in a fearless manner, built on a foundation of trust, and oriented toward helping the broader church consider how to move forward in a contentious age. I'll return to these themes in the final two chapters.

Expanding the Christian University Market

B ack in chapter 2, I examined key themes in thirty Christian university mission statements. Of the ten themes identified, seven of them focused on the nature of the environment at the school, its academic commitments, or hopes for how its graduates would shape society and the future. Taken together, these seven themes accounted for 80 percent of all themes identified.

It remains true that eighteen-to-twenty-two-year-olds are the target population of these mission commitments. While many Christian universities have branched into new program markets—including degree completion, online offerings, or graduate degrees—and argue that these are congruent with the existing mission, program expansion has required a reinterpretation of core commitments.

Students in such programs are still looking for an education that is connected to Christian values and taught by faculty members of faith. There is still a commitment to seeing leaders developed for the future. But enrollment in these programs is more likely to be related to professional advancement than the faith and character development expected by the traditional population.

Furthermore, the integration of faith and learning championed by Arthur Holmes takes on a very different character when separated from the full residential campus experience.[1] Returning to the lan-

---

1. Arthur Frank Holmes, *The Idea of a Christian College* (Grand Rapids: Eerdmans, 1975; 1987).

guage of Fischman and Gardner,[2] students in nonresidential programs are far more likely to pursue transactional educational goals than transformational ones. Students interacting in a once-a-week cohort experience or via an online discussion board have a markedly different experience than residential students.

The future vibrancy of the fearless Christian university depends upon a more robust population of traditional students—those fresh out of high school. Having more students of this type provides a buffer against some of the program reduction moves frequently in the news. The solution for Christian universities lies not in chasing the newest innovation. It rests instead in reaching populations that are not part of the normal recruiting pool.

In this chapter, I first will examine the role of demographics both in the rise of Christian universities and in contemporary challenges. The "demographic cliff" is a reality affecting all of higher education but may disproportionately affect the Christian college. Second, I explore the role played by the above-mentioned nontraditional programs as a response to perceived demographic challenges. Third, I will summarize an analysis of enrollment patterns from twenty-five Christian universities over the course of the 2010s. Fourth, I consider a variety of data about Gen Z and argue that this rising generation may in fact be more aligned with the mission of Christian universities—in spite of their reported scant religious commitments—than one might think.

A Quick Look at Demographics

Demographics has to do with the size and makeup of a population. When a population or subpopulation becomes significantly larger or smaller (due to birth rates, death rates, and migration patterns), that

2. Wendy Fischman and Howard Gardner, *The Real World of College: What Higher Education Is and What It Can Be* (Cambridge, MA: MIT Press, 2022).

change or demographic shift often has broad and long-lasting social and cultural consequences.

As the *Washington Post*'s Philip Bump notes in *The Aftermath*,[3] perhaps the best-known example of a demographic shift is the US baby boom between 1946 and 1964. The size of this group, the boomers, relative to the total population had and continues to have major implications for US society as a whole.[4]

In many ways, the baby boom is responsible for the growth of Christian liberal arts institutions across the country. New populations of potential students, especially when combined with the impact of the GI Bill, which allowed many veterans to pursue a college degree, encouraged the growth of previously sleepy institutions. More students meant competition for prestige and federal dollars, feeding a period of (regional) accreditation. The baby boom, in turn, fed programmatic growth, faculty hiring (especially those with earned doctorates), and facility expansion. Adam Laats describes this process in *Fundamentalist U*: "At the end of the war, too, the GI Bill sent millions of new students flooding onto America's college campuses, including evangelical and fundamentalist ones. By the late 1960s, rising incomes and the baby boom helped keep the postwar enrollment explosion going. In many ways, established evangelical and fundamentalist schools found themselves growing by leaps and bounds in the new environment of postwar higher education."[5]

By the late 1980s, this influx of new students had started to slow. I remember a conversation with the academic vice president of my first institution in which he raised concerns about the school's need to diversify the student body in preparation for the coming gully. It is no surprise that the boom in degree-completion programs for working adults took off in this period. This was followed by graduate programs,

---

3. Philip Bump, *The Aftermath: The Last Days of the Baby Boom and the Future of Power in America* (New York: Viking, 2023).

4. I was born almost exactly in the middle of the baby boom.

5. Adam Laats, *Fundamentalist U: Keeping the Faith in American Higher Education* (New York: Oxford University Press, 2018), 191.

first in business and education, followed by other areas to service recent graduates. Online was still decades away.

One of the dynamics of these more entrepreneurial programs was that they were highly dependent on the characteristics of the broader market. Programs for working adults (I led one in the early 1990s) depended upon students needing a college degree for advancement. A poor economy fed enrollment. A good economy hindered it.

Similarly, graduate programs in education were built around providing teachers with the necessary credentials to meet state requirements and move up on the salary scale. As states had financial difficulties, they dropped these requirements and were reluctant to incentivize pay increases. Graduate programs in education have suffered for a decade as a result.

While the good news is that this diversification provided a hedge against demographic declines, the bad news is that managing such distinct programmatic efforts seriously complicated higher education administration. A shortfall in any one of the delivery strands causes problems for the institution, often resulting in an administrative version of whack-a-mole. In good years, the diversification protected against a downturn in the traditional population. In rough years, where institutions miss targets in multiple modalities, concerns about the future become dire.

A new demographic cliff is now on the horizon.[6] A 2022 *Inside Higher Ed* article estimated that in that year there were nearly one million fewer students in college than before the COVID-19 pandemic.[7] Universities across the country are looking to reduce programs and faculty or staff positions in anticipation of this crunch. This demographic shift seems even more threatening when combined with ongoing concerns about student loan indebtedness, the proliferation of opinion pieces questioning the value of college, recent moves by states

6. Liam Knox, "Grasping for a Foothold on the Enrollment Cliff," *Inside Higher Ed*, May 12, 2023, https://tinyurl.com/4u9w4pw9.

7. Emma Whitford, "Enrollment Marches Downward," *Inside Higher Ed*, January 12, 2022, https://tinyurl.com/mpkpns2c.

to remove degree requirements for state employment, and the fact that economic data is generally good.

Shifts in religious affiliation and outlook, especially among the youngest generations, make it even harder for Christian universities to respond to the above challenges. As Robert Jones observed a decade ago in *The End of White Christian America*,[8] the combination of lower birth rates, increased immigration, and rates of religious disaffiliation has left the Protestant church in general and the evangelical church in particular in a general state of decline. Five years later, David Gushee explained further: "This disillusionment is especially a challenge for the young and those without theological education. This is because—as I often tell my ministerial students—for most people the only version of Christianity that they know about is the one we are giving them. If that one available version of the faith, *the version that we offer them*, is corrupted, then our people may naturally conclude that they had better flee before church itself damages their one and only soul."[9]

Even among those young people who have maintained deep faith commitments, things are different. At the beginning of my career, many Christian universities served as supports for their denomination. It was not uncommon for there to be a direct line from the church youth group to the summer camp experience to freshman registration at the denominational Christian school. In the intervening decades, the percentage of students and faculty affiliated with the sponsoring denomination has plummeted. As these populations become more generically evangelical (or even ecumenical), it becomes harder for the institution to retain the distinct theological identity of its past.[10]

An additional factor challenging the Christian university is cost.

8. Robert P. Jones, *The End of White Christian America* (New York: Simon and Schuster, 2015).

9. David P. Gushee, *After Evangelicalism: The Path to a New Christianity* (Louisville: Westminster John Knox Press, 2020), 27.

10. This shift has created serious challenges between denominations and their affiliated universities, as the Seattle Pacific story in the last chapter illustrated. Rethinking this relationship is the focus of chapter 8.

While institutions may heavily discount tuition through unfunded scholarships, the perceived difference in cost relative to nearby state schools or community colleges has been hard to overcome. Especially since the Great Recession of the late 2000s, parents have been increasingly likely to send their students to a less expensive community college option, perhaps transferring to the Christian university later. This becomes especially problematic for institutions where the development of faith and character is central to mission. Clearly, not as much can happen in two years as can happen in four.

Given these headwinds, both those nationally and those internal to the evangelical subculture, it is not surprising that many Christian universities have struggled in recent years. While these schools may not be closing at the rate analysts suggested some years ago,[11] many of them have dealt with complicated enrollment patterns.

A Look at Christian University Enrollments

Given the complexity of program variations described above, it can be difficult to get a sense of how enrollments shift over time. Thankfully, schools report institutional information to the Department of Education every two years, so there is a record of enrollment. This data is publicly accessible through the Integrated Postsecondary Education Data System (IPEDS).[12]

I analyzed the enrollment history from 2011 to 2019 at twenty-five CCCU institutions.[13] Most of these were also the schools included

---

11. Alliance University (formerly Nyack College) and The King's College in New York City each lost accreditation in 2023; the former closed, and the latter laid off its faculty and did not offer classes for the 2023–2024 academic year. Multnomah University became, via merger, the Multnomah campus of Jessup University on May 1, 2024. In June 2024, Eastern Nazarene College announced its closure.

12. The data may be viewed at https://nces.ed.gov/ipeds/.

13. I have opted to describe them generically rather than naming winners and losers.

in the mission analysis in chapter 2. A couple were dropped because they have enrollment caps or had significant methodological shifts during the period in question.[14] I stopped with fall 2019, avoiding the potential confounding effect of the COVID-19 crisis.

While there were a few schools that showed major enrollment shifts in the middle of the period (e.g., 2015 or 2017), most schools showed remarkable stability. Of the twenty-five schools, seven showed growth of 20 percent or more between fall 2011 and fall 2019. Four of those saw total enrollment at least double, with the largest growing by three and a half times.

At the other extreme, seven institutions lost more than 10 percent of their enrollment. Two of those lost more than 20 percent, and one more than 30 percent.

The remaining twelve schools showed minor growth (up to 15 percent) or minor loss (as much as 10 percent). Of course, the budgetary implications of even a 5 percent loss can be challenging.

Given the diversity of programming, the growth driver for many of these schools was found in graduate programming or degree-completion offerings. The latter precludes a simple undergraduate-to-graduate analysis, since they are included in undergraduate counts.

To estimate the traditional student enrollment at the institutions, I used an age breakdown available in IPEDS. It separates enrollment into those under twenty-five and those twenty-five and older. This provides a rough approximation of the traditional population (even though there may be older traditional students or younger degree-completion or graduate students).

The median institution had 65 percent of enrollment made up of traditional students. For four institutions, nontraditional students made up less than 10 percent of enrollment. At the other extreme, four had more than half of their enrollment from this population.

Some schools had very large nontraditional programs that raised the institutional profile, resulting in more traditional undergraduates.

---

14. This was the result of moving nontraditional programs into a separate organizational unit.

Three of these schools saw traditional enrollment grow by more than 70 percent over the time period.

At the other extreme, seven institutions lost at least 10 percent of their traditional students over the period. Two of these lost more than 20 percent, and one lost more than 30 percent.

It is hard to identify any predictable correlates of these institutional patterns. On the one hand, four of the seven schools with high rates of traditional growth are known as very conservative schools. Three have a national reputation. Two are in attractive locations. Two are relatively unknown outside their region.

On the other extreme, three of the seven shrinking institutions have national reputations. Four are in what could be considered destination locations. Four are known to be quite conservative in orientation.

This lack of ready correlates to growth presents serious problems for administrators, trustees, and donors. As much as it can be tempting to model an institution after a nearby conservative school big on culture wars, there is no guarantee that this is sufficient to build reputation or enrollment. Clearly, institutions are already place-bound, so being in a destination students enjoy cannot be managed, even with urban study programs.

What these institutions need is more students. The challenge over the next decade is that these students will look very different from Christian university students of the past. Reaching out to new populations of students will require rearticulating the university mission in ways that resonate with the younger generation.

One way to examine this challenge is by starting with the available population. In 2022, there were 21.6 million Americans between the ages of fifteen and nineteen, a likely target population for Christian university enrollment.[15] The most recent Census of American Religion from the Public Religion Research Institute (PRRI) shows that 9 percent of Gen Z identify as white evangelicals, the predominant

15. "Resident Population of the United States by Sex and Age as of July 1, 2022," Statista, updated October 2, 2023, https://tinyurl.com/j3a529t7.

market for Christian institutions.[16] As of 2020, the high school grad-uation rate was 87 percent.[17] Multiplying those figures leaves just un-der 1.7 million potential white evangelical students. Recent data from the Bureau of Labor Statistics reports that 62 percent of high school graduates attend college of any type.[18] Multiplying these two figures leaves just over one million potential white evangelical students. Given that we began with a five-year window of fifteen-to-nineteen-year-olds, that leaves about two hundred thousand per year. Dividing that market among the CCCU's 130 schools comes to 1,600 potential students each year, a figure about one thousand students below the median traditional enrollment of the schools in the analysis above. Given standard retention patterns year over year, most schools would need to capture roughly half the available market to achieve 2,500 students. Any serious interest overlap with state schools would make that hard to achieve.

There are not enough potential students to support the current institutions, at least using current recruiting strategies. Certainly, there will always be winners and losers in a competitive higher education market. But the gap between the haves and have-nots will only grow wider unless something changes dramatically.[19]

Institutions have attempted to respond to enrollment uncertainty in some predictable ways. They have added specialized graduate pro-grams, hoping to meet needs of the broader geographic community while tapping new markets. They have looked at the interests of tra-

16. Public Religion Research Institute, *Threats to American Democracy Ahead of an Unprecedented Presidential Election*, October 25, 2023, https://tinyurl.com/ywjt4jy2.

17. National Center for Education Statistics, *Fast Facts: High School Graduation Rates* (Washington, DC: National Center for Education Statistics, 2023).

18. US Bureau of Labor Statistics, "College Enrollment and Work Activity of Recent High School and College Graduates Summary," last modified April 26, 2023, https://tinyurl.com/3unhhwn9.

19. Robert Kelchen, "The Haves and Have-Nots of Higher Education," *Chronicle of Higher Education,* June 14, 2023, https://tinyurl.com/y4mu44yu.

ditional applicants who didn't enroll to see if they can meet a specific demand with a new program offering. They have entered into partnerships with third-party vendors to expand online offerings.

The new program initiatives prove to be riskier than they may have appeared. The new graduate program is successful until the market gets sated. The new program identified from the applicant pool proves harder to fill as student interests move to the next new thing. The third-party vendor doesn't have a deep understanding of the institutional ethos, and the online program begins to feel like a turnkey operation with little connection to mission.

Institutions have financed these initiatives by eliminating majors with low enrollment or by consolidating offerings. Faculty and staff positions are eliminated. Over time, the central focus of the institution shifts away from liberal arts and toward vocational offerings.

The long-term impact of these strategies is to weaken the "soul" of the Christian liberal arts university. Generalist faculty members are expendable in place of the specialization needed for new programs. Use of adjunct faculty increases exponentially. Students and alumni notice that the institution isn't the same as what they once thought. Retention becomes a challenge, and alumni referrals decrease, both of which only exacerbate the initial enrollment challenge.

EMBRACING THE ZOOMERS

There is another potential solution to the demographic shifts: to radically widen the recruitment pool. Rather than facing already fierce competition among the traditional evangelical market, a fearless Christian university could recognize the opportunities present among Gen Z in general. The PRRI Census of Religion mentioned above identifies an additional 17 percent of Gen Z that identifies as white mainline or Catholic. Even more significantly, 7 percent are Black Protestants, and 14 percent are either Hispanic Protestants or Hispanic Catholics.[20]

20. Public Religion Research Institute, *Threats to American Democracy*.

In his book *Fight*, Harvard researcher John Della Volpe nicknames members of Generation Z as Zoomers (a play on baby boomers as well as a reference to schooling in the COVID-19 era).[21] Zoomers, he claims, "will change America more than growing up in America will change them."[22]

Reaching this broader population presents a challenge to the regular recruiting model of many Christian universities. As Bethel University history professor Chris Gehrz suggests, it may be time for Christian universities to drop faith requirements for student admission.[23] This would not affect the Christian commitments expected of faculty and staff, curriculum requirements for Bible or theology classes, chapel expectations, or lifestyle agreements. But it would mean that incoming students would not be expected to profess Christian faith, and certainly not in recognizably evangelical terms. Most institutions have experience at this through their recruitment of athletes or reliance on commuter students. The change would present an opportunity to introduce the integration of faith and learning in new and exciting ways.

Expanding to a more diverse population would also require Christian universities to be more open on key political and social issues. Institutions that oppose DEI (diversity, equity, and inclusion) initiatives will find it hard to attract and retain students of color. Similarly, those institutions that make life uncomfortable for LGBTQ+ students will find it hard to recruit mainline students.

Retention of these more diverse populations is crucial. As hard as it might be to recruit them in the first place given the historic reputation of Christian universities, if the institution is not a welcoming place that sees diversity as a strength, those students will not only not stay but encourage peers to stay away.

21. John Della Volpe, *Fight: How Gen Z is Channeling Their Fear and Passion to Save America* (New York: St. Martin's Press, 2021).

22. Della Volpe, *Fight*, 6.

23. Chris Gehrz, "It's Time to Drop the Faith Screen," *Pietist Schoolman*, January 24, 2023, https://tinyurl.com/32t7vc6w.

Reaching out to a broader market could be revitalizing for fearless Christian universities. More than that, recent data suggests that the current generation might be more open to a residential values-based education than we might expect. A close look at this generation and the questions they are asking suggests they may be a surprisingly good match for the values of the Christian university.

Viewed in this light, Zoomers could be key to helping Christian universities move toward a fearlessness that will allow institutions to thrive. Data from several sources paint a picture of the complexity of the Zoomer experience. They may not be as evangelical as past generations, but they have a strong sense of morality. They have serious concerns about the future yet manage to maintain an overall optimism. They have doubts about institutions but are committed to making a difference in society.

Three national surveys illustrate this complexity. The Springtide Research Institute gathered data from 4,546 thirteen-to-twenty-five-year-olds in October 2022.[24] The Institute of Politics at Harvard's Kennedy School of Government conducted a survey of 2,069 eighteen-to-twenty-nine-year-olds in March 2023.[25] In January 2023, PRRI released a report on a survey oversampling Gen Z.[26] This last survey is particularly useful for my purposes, as it separates younger Zoomers (aged thirteen to seventeen) from those eighteen and over.

These surveys paint a varied picture of the religious life of Zoomers. Forty-one percent of respondents in the Harvard survey claimed to be Protestant, evangelical, Catholic, or "just Christian." Thirty-two

---

24. Springtide Research Institute, *The State of Religion & Young People 2023: Exploring the Sacred* (Winona, MN: Springtide Research Institute, 2023).

25. Institute of Politics at Harvard Kennedy School, *Survey of Young Americans' Attitudes toward Politics and Public Service, 45th edition: March 13–22, 2023*, updated April 24, 2023, https://tinyurl.com/mr33a2wf.

26. Public Religion Research Institute, *A Political and Cultural Glimpse into America's Future: Generation Z's Views on Generational Change and the Challenges and Opportunities Ahead*, January 22, 2024, https://tinyurl.com/268fx7xj.

percent claimed to be "born again." Religion is seen as somewhat or very important for nearly three-fourths of the Harvard respondents. When asked by Springtide if they felt that they were flourishing religiously or spiritually, eight in ten answered "somewhat" or "a lot." Over a third of the Springtide respondents said that they were moderately or very religious, and 45 percent said they were raised religious. Perhaps because PRRI's young Zoomers were still at home, they are 10 percent more likely to attend church and 10 percent less likely to be unaffiliated than their older peers.

At the same time, Zoomers have concerns about religion. In the Springtide survey, nearly a quarter reported having no trust in religious institutions. In the PRRI survey, the younger Gen Z respondents were 13 percent more likely to trust organized religion. Nearly half of the Harvard respondents worry about linkages between religion and government.

In response to another question, 66 percent of Springtide respondents said that they would be interested in being part of an in-person spiritual community. In *Fight,* John Della Volpe paints a picture of this religious complexity: "Although less overtly religious than any previous generation, Zoomers take more seriously the biblical admonition that if one suffers, all suffer."[27]

This concern for morality can be seen in Zoomers' frustration with the status quo. The Harvard survey found that nearly two-thirds were concerned about the moral direction of the country. It also asked a series of questions about whether respondents had trust in various institutions in society. The percentage responding that they never have faith in these institutions ranged from 20 percent (the Supreme Court) to 41 percent (Wall Street), with the president and Congress at 25 percent, and media at 40 percent. Nearly 60 percent felt that politics can't meet current challenges and that government doesn't represent American values.

27. Della Volpe, *Fight,* 46.

And yet Zoomers want to have influence. Four in ten in the Springtide survey said that they wanted to affect society, and six in ten wanted to help others.

The Zoomers in the surveys are also dealing with personal challenges. Over half of the Harvard respondents reported being nervous or anxious for several days over the previous two weeks. Four in ten reported feeling lonely or afraid over the course of several recent days.

Despite this, Zoomers are an optimistic bunch. A CBS News/YouGov poll from September 2023 found that eighteen-to-twenty-nine-year-olds were significantly more optimistic in their view of the state of the country, the economy, and even climate than any of the other cohorts polled.[28] Here's Della Volpe again: "In just a handful of years, Zoomers have taken on the most imperishable and destructive forces holding our country back from meeting its undeniable promise. They do so with their voices, their homemade signs, their memes, their ballots, and their wallets. Because they have no choice. With an unparalleled knowledge of history and science for their age, they are filled with fear but using it to find the courage that propels their lives and this era in our nation forward."[29]

But what does this mass of data mean for the fearless Christian university as it reaches out to Zoomers in all their complexity? And why should Zoomers care about Christian universities?

I gave an answer to the first question earlier in the chapter: Christian universities should reach out to Zoomers because that is their stated mission. The most common mission theme from the review of Christian university mission in chapter 2 was the development of future leaders that will shape a changing society.

As John Della Volpe's book covers in depth, many Zoomers already see themselves as shaping society. He provides a detailed look at the leaders of the March for Our Lives protest prompted by the

28. YouGov, "CBS News Poll – September 5–8, 2023," updated September 8, 2023, https://tinyurl.com/3zx38tke.

29. Della Volpe, *Fight*, 186–87.

2018 shootings at Marjory Stoneman Douglas High School in Parkland, Florida. Two of those leaders, David Hogg and Maxwell Frost, are already having a massive impact on American politics. Hogg has founded a pro-democracy super PAC, and Frost is the first Zoomer elected to Congress. In Tennessee, two young Black state representatives who were removed from their seats by the Republican majority (but later reinstated by voters) for protesting gun violence after a school shooting are both Zoomers.[30]

Rather than hoping that Christian university graduates might someday be shapers of society, it would be far better for those institutions to be a safe place for those already trying to have an impact in their world. Inviting those students in will mean that institutions will have to become more open to contentious conversations on race and politics and climate, but that should really be a part of institutional identity anyway.

A second major theme in the review of Christian university missions was a commitment to being a holistic Christian community. Such communities are welcoming places for students from a variety of backgrounds and experiences. They turn diversity into a strength, as students, faculty, staff, and administration learn to navigate existing differences and similarities. Broadening the scope of institutional diversity beyond a predominantly evangelical population increases the vitality of a community. The institution can express its Christian ethos to a broader range of students, perhaps enlivening long-dormant religious beliefs and practices. This will require the institution not to make assumptions about the depth of religious knowledge present among its students, but that too is something they should be doing already.

The third major theme in Christian university mission concerned academic excellence. Chapter 3 argued that the academic focus of a fearless Christian university should be on the lived experience, ques-

---

30. Bill Chappell and Vanessa Romo, "Tennessee House Votes to Expel 2 of 3 Democratic Members over Gun Protest," NPR, April 6, 2023, https://tinyurl.com/5n7ybe7b.

tions, and fears of the students. As they pursue their coursework and majors, they should be undergoing the kind of transformational learning characteristic of a Christian liberal arts institution.

The research on Zoomers shows that they have concerns about a host of issues within broader society. They believe that critical issues should be addressed. As John Della Volpe said on a November 2023 podcast, "members of Generation Z are interested in policy, not just opinion."[31] A current Christian university student captured this sentiment well by referring to a slogan on a t-shirt worn by students at her public high school after national news of another school shooting or racial incident: "Nothing changes if nothing changes."[32]

Having a broader array of Zoomers in classes at Christian universities expands not only an institution's numbers but the academic horizons of the more traditional evangelical student. And, even more than that, it can benefit this broader group of Gen Z students too. Although the public reputation of many Christian universities might make this difficult for them to see, a fearless institution can potentially articulate a sense of welcome and desire for wholeness that these students might find very attractive.

Each of these three Christian university mission components meets felt needs of the Zoomers in the surveys summarized earlier. Consider the role of developing future leaders. Zoomers are more optimistic than earlier generations. That optimism can be a wonderful starting place for a meaningful consideration of the major social issues students might affect as graduates. As they already have a bias toward addressing such issues, they are a great match for the culture-making approach discussed at the end of chapter 4.

The Zoomers' need for belonging and acceptance matches up with the self-identification of the Christian university as a Christ-centered

31. Jon Favreau, Jon Lovett, Dan Pfeiffer, and Tommy Vietor, hosts, "First Rule of Republican Fight Club," November 16, 2023, in *Pod Save America*, produced by Crooked Media, podcast, https://tinyurl.com/2kewkxva.

32. Anna Mares, interview with the author, December 4, 2023.

community. The data indicates the great anxiety and sense of isolation that many Zoomers experience. Without denying the value of connections to others via social media, institutions can provide the kind of communal support and face-to-face engagement that may help ease the fears and concerns of many Zoomers.

The academic life of the Christian university also matches up well with Zoomer concerns and needs. They want a way to address key questions of the day. If they cannot do that within the higher ed options available to them, they will do it by relying on YouTube. Far better, however, would be to invite them into a well-grounded approach to scholarly resources.

But the liberal arts are not just key to academic mission. They also go a long way toward enhancing democratic discourse. Another area ripe for expansion is for students to develop a better sense of the proper place of institutions in society. The data shows that a significant percentage of students lack trust in a variety of social institutions. Insights from sociology, history, political science, and philosophy would go a long way to restore trust in institutions. However, these are precisely the programs that many colleges are reducing or eliminating in pursuit of more vocationally oriented programs. But bringing questions about the place and trustworthiness of institutions to the center of university life could provide an enrollment boost that would make these beleaguered programs more robust.

Appealing to a broader array of Generation Z students strengthens the core mission of the fearless Christian university in ways that degree-completion or graduate programs cannot. Rather than simply being a "safe place" for evangelical students to get an education that doesn't disrupt their prior commitments, the fearless Christian university has the potential to be a center of social and cultural exploration within the context of its Christian ethos. Although he is not talking about Christian universities in particular, John Della Volpe offers a hopeful vision at the end of *Fight* that I fully share: "I cannot wait for the day when I walk into a room of young people, ask them how their life and our country are going and, rather than hearing tales of fear and despair, I'm overwhelmed with accounts of faith and progress. I have a feeling those days might come sooner than we think."[33]

There is one additional advantage to the fearless Christian university embracing a wider population of Zoomers. It would allow the institution to become a laboratory of navigating generational change, thereby benefiting faculty, staff, administrators, trustees, and donors. The more university leaders engage with students and their concerns, the better prepared those leaders are to guide their institutions into a fearless future. That golden opportunity is the topic of the next chapter.

33. Della Volpe, *Fight*, 206.

Listening to the New Generation

Selecting which college to attend is always a leap of faith for an eighteen-year-old. Even if parents or siblings or friends attended one's school of choice, knowing how the decision will play out over four years is impossible.

Perusing a Christian university website doesn't give as much information as one might want. A quick examination of half a dozen admissions pages reveals a very similar pattern. On the landing page there are between six and ten smiling students, many in university-branded attire, looking like they really enjoy each other's company. Of course, they were likely rounded up by an admissions photographer and may not even know each other. There will be an appropriate balance of females to males, roughly matching the gender ratio of the school. There will be one or two students of color (overrepresenting their proportion of the student body).

There will be the requisite chapel photo, perhaps showing the student band leading worship while other students stand with their arms raised to heaven. There will be the classroom photo showing a faculty member lecturing or leading a discussion while an eager student raises her hand to contribute. Of course, sports photos are a must as a way of illustrating school pride.

The new student no doubt knows that many of these photos are staged and don't exactly reflect the daily lived experience of students who attend this particular Christian university. Nevertheless, these images are important in setting expectations for the idealized Christian university student. Those images of happy, sociable, inquisitive, spiritual students have an impact on how new students come to see themselves.

There are, of course, students on campus who closely match the images promoted in the admissions brochures. They are the ones who are most likely to be invited to meet the trustees, to hang around the chaplain's office, to run for student government, or to sit with the college president at the basketball game. It is far too easy for administrators and trustees to think that those students are representative of the student body as a whole rather than a self-selected group.

I have argued for embracing the diversity of Gen Z students as a key strategy to avoid the doomsday scenarios of the impending demographic cliff and perhaps arrest the program cutting that is rife within Christian universities. We can now take that argument a step farther, exploring the ways in which understanding Gen Z can empower administrators and trustees to better prepare for the next decade of Christian higher education. Institutions that move to embrace this generation of students and trust their judgment will position themselves as fearless Christian universities that can move well beyond culture wars.

How Students Really Are

Seeing these students in their complexity will require institutions to move well beyond the wholesome smiling faces that adorn admissions brochures and web pages. Being a holistic Christian community requires accepting students where they are, struggles and all, and not expecting they be the idealized version of Christian college students we advertise and highlight.

Three anecdotes set the stage for this argument. The first comes from the beginning of my teaching career, and the second from the end. The third was from a recent interview with a current Christian university student.

In my first institution, I taught the research methods course for the MBA program. One of the students worked in the admissions department and was interested in exploring whether alumni parents had a preference to send their kids to their alma mater. Her advisor told me that she had completed her surveys and found that parents felt that their own children had been sufficiently grounded in the faith to attend the well-known state school. However, as one set of parents noted, there was a teen in the church youth group who would really benefit. That teen was new to faith, from a family of divorce, and had past issues with drug use. While that student never enrolled, as far as I know, the image of a student with such baggage has remained with me. By no means the prototypical Christian university freshman, such a student would challenge numerous assumptions about the university student experience, to say nothing of the supports necessary for that student to thrive.

The second anecdote comes from my last semester of college teaching, the spring of 2020. That was the semester when COVID-19 disrupted everything in higher education and shifted teaching from a small classroom setting to Zoom instruction with students sitting on their beds trying hard to pay attention. One of my students stands out in my memory. First, she got Covid herself and took a while to recover, falling behind in her work. Then Covid restrictions prompted an elderly relative with mental health issues to move into her home. As her mother was still at work trying to keep things together, it fell to my student to provide care for her elderly relative. Her work suffered because of these competing demands.

I don't have specific statistics, but anecdotally I can attest that what was a rare occurrence in the 1980s—a student with lots of baggage coming to the Christian university—had become far more common by 2020. Today's students are dealing with more issues. It may be family discord, sexual abuse, illness (their own or a loved one's), sexual orientation and gender identity, ADHD diagnoses, bipolar struggles, depression, eating disorders, racial animosity, and more. This is on top of the normal adjustments of college life: dealing with roommates, romantic relationships, classroom adjustments, and the like. Moreover, today's students are more likely to be very open about their past and present struggles.

That brings me to the third anecdote. In a recent conversation, the Christian university student mentioned in the previous chapter told a story of a friend who had confided to her that she had suffered a complete mental breakdown in middle school. This significant challenge was simply a part of her friend's biography, like what town she was born in. It may be that there were similar issues among students in earlier decades and now they are simply more willing to discuss them, but nevertheless it is clear that Christian universities cannot ignore these stories.

Trustees and administrators may not know the challenges that students face.[1] Frankly, unless faculty members build an intentional bridge to their students, it is far too easy for them to remain unaware.

The students who regularly interact with trustees and administrators look far more like the admissions photos than the student body at large. That's not to point fingers. Little of the work of administrators involves the rank-and-file student body. Even interactions with student leaders can occur in a somewhat guarded environment. I loved getting to know student leaders in my administrative days, but it was hard to know them well. Even open conversation over meals was not enough. And the challenge is even greater for trustees who are on campus for only a couple of days two to three times a year.

Navigating the next decade of Christian higher education will require administrators and trustees to take a far broader view of the student experience. They need to prepare the institution for a far more complex understanding of everything: personal crises, politics, diversity, and faith development. It will require a deeper embrace of what it means for the Christian university to be values driven, not in the culture-war sense but as a celebration of the core identity of the institution.

---

1. Public Religion Research Institute (PRRI), *A Political and Cultural Glimpse into America's Future: Generation Z's Views on Generational Change and the Challenges and Opportunities Ahead*, January 22, 2024, https://tinyurl.com/268fx7xj. This survey found that nearly 60 percent of younger Gen Zs felt that older generations did not understand their struggles.

John Della Volpe, whose book *Fight* I introduced in the previous chapter, outlines the challenge well: "Generation Z is asking us every day to have the honest and difficult conversations about politics, race, culture, our history, and future that too many parents and school jurisdictions are unwilling to tackle."[2] The fearless Christian university not only is willing to have these difficult conversations but sees such dialogues as central to its overall mission.

ADMINISTRATORS AND TRUSTEES COMMUNICATING TO STUDENTS

Today's students are skeptical of institutions in general. In part, this arises from a sense that institutions are not functioning to effectively address the critical issues of concern to Zoomers.

This is true of higher education as well. A summer 2023 Gallup survey reported that Americans' confidence in colleges and universities had fallen since 2015. Whereas 57 percent of respondents reported having a "great deal" or "quite a lot" of confidence in 2015,[3] only 36 percent reported the same in 2023.[4] The drop is similar for the youngest cohort in the Gallup results. Among eighteen-to-thirty-four-year-olds,[5] confidence in higher education fell from 60 percent to 42 percent.

The Gallup survey did not explore the reasons for the decline, but the report suggested concerns about college costs, which likely includes concern over potential student loan debt. It is quite likely that

2. John Della Volpe, *Fight: How Gen Z Is Channeling Their Fear and Passion to Save America* (New York: St. Martin's Press, 2021), 110–11.

3. The PRRI survey mentioned above (*Political and Cultural Glimpse into America's Future*) found that 56 percent of young Gen Z respondents think college is a good investment.

4. Megan Brenan, "Americans' Confidence in Higher Education Down Sharply," Gallup, July 11, 2023, https://tinyurl.com/5u8j4ty7.

5. It would be helpful if all the major polling agencies agreed upon standard age categories!

the negative coverage of issues in higher education from the media and conservative politicians and pundits has fed this distrust. There is a distinct partisan difference in the Gallup results, with Democrats' support dropping by 9 percent and Republicans' support dropping by a whopping 37 percent!

While it's hard to be specific about how student attitudes at Christian universities align with those of the general population, it's reasonable to assume that their level of concern is similar. They need regular reassurance that the educational choice they have made—to attend a Christian college—was worthwhile.

Too often, the case for attending a Christian university is shared only at freshman orientation and commencement. Even then, it is often presented in contrast to the more secular wing of higher education, with a focus on what's wrong with other places and not on the values that drive Christian institutions. Students at Christian universities need to be reassured that their institution is committed to its complex mission and not simply operating as a business enterprise. They should know that what happens to them day in and day out is central to what the Christian university is all about.

Like trustees, students often are unaware of the inner workings of the university. They go to class, to chapel, and to the dining hall and may have well-formed positions for and against certain practices, but they don't know how administrators make decisions or what variables and priorities they are considering. If students were brought into these decision-making processes, life would be better for campus leaders.

As Della Volpe observes, "Generation Z recognized and voiced more quickly than others that it was structural deficiencies in our institutions, and not any one individual, that were to blame for the position in which they, and our nation, now find themselves."[6] Properly informed students may be far less likely to lay blame at the feet of the college president.

Furthermore, students need to hear the value of the liberal arts and critical thinking extolled by university leaders. Depending upon their

6. Della Volpe, *Fight*, 34.

own educational and professional background, trustees themselves may first need to have these values rehearsed. But administrators should regularly demonstrate to students that they fully endorse the university's commitment to the liberal arts even in the face of difficult issues. Covenant College philosophy professor Kelly Kapic argued this in a *Christianity Today* essay:

> At a Christian liberal arts college, we wrestle with the hard questions (not always solving them!), while applying to these challenges the faith handed down through the ages. We seek not easy answers but slow-growing wisdom and the formation of godly instincts. One of the most important things Christian faculty members at any institution can do is believe. Students witness thoughtful professors who don't have all the answers, who are honest about the real challenges, who delight in insights from whatever source (including non-Christians), and in it all, the professor still stands there believing.[7]

While Kapic focuses on faculty, I would argue that this is even more significant for administrators. They must demonstrate intellectual humility while seriously engaging student questions and concerns.

When administrators reduce liberal arts programs in favor of more vocational majors in service of hoped-for financial stability, they communicate to students that the liberal arts and critical thinking components of institutional identity are just nice words. When these shifts are explained using cold business rationales (number of majors, small percentage of students affected), students rightly see this as a dodge.

Most importantly, students need administrators and trustees to see them as they are. In my conversations with recent Christian university grads, far too many have said they felt they had to struggle to fit in. That struggle was so hard that many now seriously question whether

7. Kelly M. Kapic, "The Power of the Christian Quad," *Christianity Today* 63, no. 8 (October 2019): 40–44.

they would do it again if given the chance. Low enrollment is already a challenge, and these are not the kinds of student outcomes that will foster enthusiastic referrals. If, on the other hand, these students had felt that they were accepted as they are in the spirit of Christian community, they would likely commend the institution to others even if they disagreed with administrators or trustees on specific matters.

STUDENTS COMMUNICATING TO ADMINISTRATORS AND TRUSTEES

As much as students of all types can benefit from true engagement with administrators and trustees, the value of those interactions for the administrators and trustees is even greater. Given the ways Zoomers differ from these older institutional leaders, it is critical that the latter not try to replicate their own experiences. Here is John Della Volpe again:

> A values-based ideological gap that divides Americans by year of birth, mostly nonexistent in 2000, is now a driving force in local and national political contests. Every day younger and older Americans wake up to different Americas. Many older people still see their country as the "shining city on a hill" that Puritan John Winthrop envisioned almost four hundred years ago and that twentieth-century presidents John F. Kennedy and Ronald Reagan invoked at key junctures in their political careers. The coming-of-age experiences of Generation Z, on the other hand, marked by rising inequality, discrimination, an endangered environment, and a fractured politics, comprise a conscious rejection of American exceptionalism.[8]

Even though Christian university students may be more conservative than their Zoomer peers, those coming-of-age experiences still

8. Della Volpe, *Fight*, 11–12.

resonate. Administrators and trustees of a fearless Christian university must regularly grapple with those experiences to effectively lead the institution both now and into the future.

If these university leaders ask today's students what they are concerned about, there is a short list of expected answers. The cost of education is high. They are worried about finding a good job after college. They are working too many hours while going to school. They aren't getting enough sleep. There isn't enough parking close to campus. The food in the dining hall could be better.

This script is well known by all parties. It's what students are expected to say. It's what the leaders have heard in scores of earlier conversations. What's remarkable about the standard script is that there is nothing the administrators and trustees can do about these particular issues.

Tuition costs are not going down. The job market is beyond institutional control. There will never be enough parking. Mass-produced food in the dining hall will always be lacking, even given the most innovative food service managers.

The deep conflicts students face will only come to light in the context of a serious relationship. It is only when they feel safe that they can expose their real struggles. It requires a trusting connection to admit that you're worried about your parents' marriage, that your sibling is struggling with drugs or alcohol, that your local church has become a haven of Christian Nationalism, that you're a closeted gay student worried about being disowned by parents, that you feel isolated on campus as a person of color, or that you've been a victim of sexual harassment by a boyfriend at home, a fellow student, or even a faculty member.

It's true that many of these issues are also beyond institutional control. But if a Christian university is true to its values, it is a community that provides support to students who struggle. These largely external issues are major factors predicting attrition early in the college experience. Therefore, being a supportive community is not only central to the institutional ethos but potentially a way to enhance the school's financial strength.

Moreover, the images of contemporary students in the public imagination primarily come from media stories, usually about a select number of students at elite universities.[9] It is easy to generalize and rely on stereotypes when thinking about today's students. The antidote to such generalization is to know actual stories of real students.

When policy discussions occur at a cabinet meeting or a board meeting, they should be informed by the actual experience of students at the university. Rather than imagining hypothetical scenarios, leaders can build an inductive sense of the concerns of actual students.

Such a specific focus makes it less likely that the leaders will get pulled into culture-war discourse. It's one thing to rail against "transgenderism." It's much more difficult to balance the university mission with concern for a specific student suffering from gender dysphoria.

Giving students a safe and trustworthy place to tell their stories allows them to live more comfortably in the Christian university and helps the leadership balance student concerns with institutional mission. Students have little interest in the latest culture-war battles. They understand the institutional commitments but want the space to be who they are.

Rather than depending upon the never-ending boundary-maintenance efforts of culture wars, institutional leaders can rely on compassion and empathy held toward actual students. This allows the institution to remain centered on its core identity, ethos, and mission.

Keeping the Mission Central

As we saw in chapter 2, most Christian university mission statements are focused on what happens to students either during their time at

9. As I write this, the public is in an uproar over a small number of pro-Palestinian students making outrageous comments around Israel's response to the Hamas attack on Israel on October 7, 2023. Although only a small number of students at a few institutions have made these comments, these public voices have taken it as an occasion to ask, What's wrong with students today?

the institution or thereafter. The more administrators, trustees, and faculty interact with students amid their complex lives, the better the values of the university can be aligned with actual practice.

In *Gay on God's Campus*, sociologist Jonathan Coley describes how Belmont University used its core values to address the question of LGBTQ+ support.[10] Even though Belmont has separated from the Tennessee Baptist Convention (a very contentious process), it still embraces an identity as a Christian university. It has grown dramatically and gained a national reputation for hosting a McCain-Obama 2008 presidential debate. As Coley notes, "More than a few observers argued that Belmont was in the midst of an identity crisis, torn between its identity as a growing nationally recognized university with a highly visible music business school, which placed it in a league of universities that generally embraced LGBT students, and its identity as a Christian university in the South, which placed it in a group of universities that generally discriminated against LGBT students."[11]

Near the end of 2010, a soccer coach in a same-sex relationship told her team that she was leaving Belmont. The campus LGBTQ+ group (Bridge Builders) launched small protests claiming that the school had forced her out. Coley writes: "The students realized that one of their most important tasks would be to frame LGBT inclusion as a Christian value, and so pro-LGBT religious signs emerged as an early theme of the protests, with students holding up signs such as 'WWJD?' (What Would Jesus Do?), 'Jesus Loves [the coach],' 'God is Love, 1 John 4:8,' 'Belmont, Love Thy Neighbor as Thyself,' and 'Jesus Had 2 Dads and He Turned Out Just Fine.' The protest was covered by Nashville's newspapers and local news stations."[12]

This embrace of the institutional mission began to have an impact. Coley quotes one student in Bridge Builders as follows: "The fact that

10. Jonathan S. Coley, *Gay on God's Campus: Mobilizing for LGBT Equality at Christian Colleges and Universities* (Chapel Hill: University of North Carolina Press, 2018).

11. Coley, *Gay on God's Campus*, 95.

12. Coley, *Gay on God's Campus*, 97–98.

Belmont is a Christian university affected how we approached the protest and also how we responded to the media. For example, we wanted to say, we love Belmont because it's supposed to be a Christian school, and we just feel like what they're doing right now has kind of strayed from the path of a Christian. You're supposed to love others and treat others as they want to be treated. So Belmont right now isn't acting like a Christian university."[13]

Interpreting the institution's Christian identity back to its leaders was important. Students and alumni wrote emails opposing the firing of the soccer coach. Faculty members were similarly supportive. But Coley highlights the especially influential role played by Belmont donor and former trustee Mike Curb, founder of the record label Curb Records, who issued statements saying, "It's time for Belmont to change" and "I promise you, if the matter is not resolved, I will continue speaking out about this the rest of my life."[14]

In January 2011, the board of trustees used the language of Christian identity to change Belmont's nondiscrimination policy. In subsequent years, the relationship between Belmont's identity as a Christian university and its engagement with LGBTQ+ students and staff became more intertwined.

The point here is that it was a dialogue between administrators, trustees, and concerned students focused on the meaning of the Christian university that shifted the dynamics on campus. Belmont, in centering its understanding of Christian community, met student concerns without falling into culture-war traps.

If Christian university mission statements focus on issues of holistic growth, leadership development, Christian community, and academic rigor, then it follows that robust discussions about what those various components imply for students, trustees, and other stakeholders are essential. Navigating the diverse perceptions of those mission components provides the fearless Christian university with a set of

13. Coley, *Gay on God's Campus*, 98.
14. Coley, *Gay on God's Campus*, 98.

tools to meet the needs of current and future students while anchoring discussions in the ethos of the institution.

Additionally, having institutions that can draw upon their Christian communal ethos to negotiate diverse views peaceably goes a long way toward rebutting claims that the Christian university is out of touch, denies academic freedom, or (in the case above) is homophobic. Relying on core institutional values can provide a helpful model for institutions wrestling with freedom of expression on topics where views within the school may differ sharply.

THE FUTURE, NOT THE PAST

The fearless Christian university that keeps the current and future students in mind is always reimagining what it means to be a faithful institution for years into the future. Listening to current students keeps the institution freshly interpreting its mission and ethos in ways that articulate continuity with the past without being stuck there.

A Christian university that maintains these ongoing commitments does not need to worry about accusations from gatekeepers that somehow it is "becoming liberal." If changes in perspectives are pursued out of service to the real needs of students being served, that is not a loss of direction. It is a reaffirmation of what the institution has always been in the context of the struggles of current students.

To take such a position changes the definition of what Christian higher education is all about. Rather than worrying about culture wars and placating those stakeholders opposed to change, the fearless Christian university can lean into its mission-based commitment to providing students with the building blocks necessary for them to thrive intellectually, spiritually, and socially as mature adults.

Pursuing these commitments will require a shift in understanding between the university and its sponsoring denomination (if it has one) and dominant feeder churches and schools. That new understanding will recognize the difference between a local church and a university.

It not only changes how the church writ large sees the institution but establishes a new and productive relationship between the church and the fearless Christian university. Unpacking that new relationship is the focus of the next chapter.

The Christian University as a Mission Outpost

The embrace of a new generation of students, a commitment to culture making instead of culture warring, and improved relationships between administrators, trustees, and faculty goes a long way toward changing the face of Christian higher education.

Yet, one final shift is necessary. Sponsoring denominations, major churches, evangelical gatekeepers, and the general public need to reimagine the central role of these institutions. This shift will alleviate the fear that has hindered Christian universities for far too long.

As Peter Berger has noted, plausibility structures are malleable. Understandings can be revised, and new ideas incorporated. In all likelihood, various stakeholders are simply perpetuating prior understandings, especially if they are Christian university alumni. Given the popular attacks on all higher education as "woke," too expensive, and not worthwhile, a certain suspicion is to be expected—unless, of course, steps are taken to change those preconceptions.

Not a Church

Central to changing our conception of the Christian university is abandoning the analogy mentioned in chapter 5—namely, that a Christian university is like a church. Too many denominations and gatekeepers have been operating in boundary-maintenance mode, trying to keep universities (and churches) in line. Because of official or implicit support, the Christian university is seen as an extension of the church's work.

When Arthur Holmes wrote his classic *The Idea of a Christian College* nearly five decades ago, he did far more than introduce the phrase "the integration of faith and learning." He was very clear that the Christian college was *not* the church. Early in the book, he writes:

> A frequent idea people have of the Christian college has been captured in the label "defender of the faith." Though defending the faith was certainly an apostolic responsibility, it is hard to extend it to all of the educational task, all of art and science or all of campus life. Yet a defensive mentality is still common among pastors and parents; many suppose that the Christian college exists to protect young people against the sin and heresy in other institutions. The idea therefore is not so much to educate as to indoctrinate, to provide a safe environment plus all the answers to all the problems posed by all the critics of orthodoxy and virtue.[1]

Holmes recognized that there is much more to Christian higher education than chapel and required Bible classes. The vision of the Christian university he shares is not only far broader than this but feeds directly into the future-leadership ethos we have seen so many institutions embrace.

> The potential of Christian higher education is inspiring. I dream about Christian college students and their future roles in life. I dream of those who go on to graduate school to teach at the college level, and I see them as a generation of Christian scholars and teachers strategically located in the colleges and universities of this and other lands, penetrating the thought-patterns of their culture with Christian beliefs and values. I dream of those who go into law and medicine, into business and education, into the armed forces, into government, into marriage, and I envision their

1. Arthur Frank Holmes, *The Idea of a Christian College* (Grand Rapids: Eerdmans, 1975; 1987), 4.

influence in reviving the Christian foundations of Western society. I dream of those who go on to seminary to preach and teach the Word of God and I pray that they may bring to the church a new sense of relevance.[2]

Why have so many Christian universities missed these admonitions from Holmes? Even today, admissions tours make a priority of including robust chapel services with specially selected preachers to excite prospective students about the vibrant spiritual life of the campus. Promotional brochures show students in residence hall Bible studies. Recruiting at teen church camps is common, and many students come with the expectation that college will be just like camp.

Many institutions failed to embrace Holmes's vision of broad and varied societal influence, gravitating instead toward a narrower, and increasingly politicized, culture-war stance. A tremendous amount of scholarship has demonstrated the ways in which the rise of the Moral Majority and Focus on the Family shifted evangelical consciousness toward political engagement and culture wars.[3] Jerry Falwell Sr. founded the Moral Majority at the US bicentennial in 1976, with Focus launching the next year.[4] This politicization of evangelicalism dwarfed the educational vision that Holmes had put forth.

The culture-war understanding became entrenched in the identity of Christian universities. Even though very few institutions defined their mission around these battles, their perception of success depended upon holding the line against broader cultural changes.

Christian universities, then, often combine an external stance of worry about culture wars with an internal stance prioritizing pietistic

---

2. Holmes, *Idea*, 41–42.

3. See, for example, Frances FitzGerald, *The Evangelicals: The Struggle to Shape America* (New York: Simon and Schuster, 2017); James Davison Hunter, *Culture Wars: The Struggle to Define America* (New York: Basic Books, 1991).

4. Tim Alberta, *The Kingdom, the Power, and the Glory: American Evangelicals in an Age of Extremism* (New York: HarperCollins, 2023).

personal faith.[5] These self-understandings are deeply grounded within the institutions. Changing them will be difficult but not impossible.

A Note on Institutions

In *Playing God*, Andy Crouch provides a good sociological treatment of institutions. He argues that "the recipe for an institution, then, is four ingredients plus three generations: artifacts, arenas, rules and roles that are passed on to the founding generation's children's children."[6]

Following his analysis, we can see Christian universities demonstrating these four ingredients. The artifacts are things I just mentioned: chapel, Bible studies, prayer before class, and much more. The arenas are places where university life is worked out: chapel, the classroom, the residence hall, the dining hall, the athletic field.[7] Rules are central to life in the Christian university. Most have some form of "lifestyle agreement" that proscribes unacceptable behaviors like drinking, smoking, drugs, or premarital sex.[8] Roles are what we discussed in chapters 5 and 7: students, faculty, administrators, trustees, denominational leaders.

If those four ingredients are oriented toward conflict, then it is hard for the institution to change toward culture making. The process of institutionalization creates a subjective, taken-for-granted, cognitive structure. Even imagining alternatives is very difficult, and shifting institutional thinking takes significant work.

Crouch's three-generation argument provides some insight into the changing nature of the current student body. A generation is

5. Chris Gehrz, ed., *The Pietist Vision of Christian Higher Education: Forming Whole and Holy Persons* (Downers Grove, IL: IVP Academic, 2014).

6. Andy Crouch, *Playing God: Redeeming the Gift of Power* (Downers Grove, IL: Intervarsity Press, 2013), 178.

7. Sociologist Pierre Bourdieu called all of these "fields," actually drawing upon the athletic comparison.

8. These lifestyle agreements also have positive prescriptions, but students rarely focus on these.

generally assumed to be fifteen to twenty years. Three generations, then, would be between forty-five and sixty years. That is precisely the span from when Holmes wrote his book (1975) and the Moral Majority took the stage (1976) to the present generation. As I've argued throughout the book, things are changing among students in this third generation, but institutions are not keeping up.

When institutions like Christian universities keep operating in ways that worked in the past even though circumstances have changed both inside and outside the school, they become what Crouch calls "zombie institutions." These are institutions that continue to do things as they always have, without a clear sense of why. It is simply a case of institutional momentum. Crouch writes: "Zombie institutions are institutions that have not faced the truth about their own failure. And because of their access to privilege—their ability to continue collecting rent—they continue to exist, crowding out institutions that might create true shalom. Zombie institutions are dedicated first and foremost to their own preservation, not to anyone's flourishing."[9] He uses churches as an example, but these comments about zombie churches are apt for Christian universities: "But over time the imperatives of self-preservation can create a risk-averse culture that prevents continued learning and growth. Zombie churches exist to keep the lights on rather than to be the light in dark places; they turn inward rather than outward; they serve insiders and ignore outsiders."[10]

Those in control often prefer to make sure the Christian university has continuity with its past. When that past orientation becomes paramount, the institution is living in its past glory while failing to address its future potential. It becomes focused on survival above all.

Tim Alberta's *The Kingdom, the Power, and the Glory* includes a chapter on Liberty University. While the national news about the fall of Jerry Falwell Jr. is well known, Alberta focuses more on the ways in which Liberty has strayed from a central academic mission. He quotes a former faculty member and alum: "'Liberty's goal has never been some holistic vision of Christian academics. It's about maximum effi-

9. Crouch, *Playing God*, 199.
10. Crouch, *Playing God*, 200.

ciency, maximum productivity, maximum profit making,' he told me. 'In that sense, Ron [Godwin] was actually establishing a continuity between Jerry Sr. and Jerry Jr. Their visions were the same. How can we make more money? How can we build a bigger institution? How can we gain political power and influence? How can we impose our conservative values on the nation?'"[11]

Revitalizing zombie institutions requires new analogies that embrace the core purpose of the institution. New images feed brave understandings. Arthur Holmes recognized the need to embrace core purposes: "I think rather that the Christian college has not sufficiently articulated its educational philosophy, and has not sold the evangelical public or perhaps even its own students and teachers on what it is trying to do."[12] He adds: "It is time that evangelical educators took the initiative in educating the evangelical public as to the nature of Christian higher education and the role of academic freedom. A college is not the church. The educator's speeches and sermons and articles as well as the college's advertisements and brochures could expound more eloquently than they do the idea of a Christian college and the responsible use to which it tries to put its freedom."[13]

If the analogy of the Christian university as church isn't sufficient, what could take its place? I suggest that there is another image within the evangelical tradition that better fits the university. That image is the mission outpost.

The Mission Outpost

The idea of a mission outpost fosters thoughts of a brave preacher taking the gospel to unreached tribes. The missionary family comes home on deputation tours to tell stories of sharing the faith with others, often with great flourish, as part of generating their support. Evangelical

11. Alberta, *Kingdom*, 403.
12. Holmes, *Idea*, 10.
13. Holmes, *Idea*, 75.

churches have been steeped in stories like that of Jim Elliot, who was killed taking the gospel to a previously unreached people group.

The actual work is far more complex. It includes those teaching English in a country closed to mission work[14] or those working within the United States with refugee populations.[15] Mission work also involves specific institutional activity. Mission organizations operate orphanages, hospitals, schools, social service agencies, and construction operations. Each of these have a Christian identity and generally hire people who are committed Christians.

David Swartz's history of World Vision, *Facing West*, documents its transition from an American evangelistic operation into a multinational partnership addressing both personal and structural needs.[16] The now-retired president of the organization, Richard Stearns, recounts his own shift from a corporate to a global perspective and calls for evangelicals to broaden their understanding of the gospel to include structural as well as individual concerns.[17]

What distinguishes this broader sort of mission outpost is that it is concerned with the common good and not simply boundary maintenance. As James Davison Hunter argues in *To Change the World*, "if there are benevolent consequences of our engagement with the world, in other words, it is precisely because it is not rooted in a desire to change the world for the better but rather because it is an expression of a desire to honor the creator of all goodness, beauty, and truth, a manifestation of our loving obedience to God and a fulfillment of God's command to love our neighbor."[18]

---

14. Amy Peterson, *Dangerous Territory: My Misguided Quest to Save the World* (Grand Rapids: Discovery House, 2017).

15. D. L. Mayfield, *Assimilate or Go Home: Notes from a Failed Missionary on Rediscovering Faith* (New York: HarperCollins, 2016).

16. David R. Swartz, *Facing West: American Evangelicals in an Age of World Christianity* (New York: Oxford University Press, 2020).

17. Richard Stearns, *The Hole in Our Gospel: The Answer That Changed My Life and Might Just Change the World* (Nashville: Thomas Nelson, 2009).

18. James Davison Hunter, *To Change the World: The Irony, Tragedy, and*

The fearless Christian university is a mission outpost. It is the place where the faith commitments of the church meet the educational needs of a variety of students. It is the place where the hard work of discerning the culture is done, to the benefit of the church in particular and the culture in general. It is forward thinking and not fighting yesterday's battles. It is unafraid of critiques from the church because its work is different from the church's. Toward the end of *Facing West*, David Swartz challenges Christian faculty to use their professional expertise to enhance the common good: "The 'scandal of the evangelical mind' posited by Mark Noll in 1994 has become less scandalous as professors have become more productive, but it has also widened the chasm between elites and a vast grassroots subculture. In order to bridge this divide, professors James K. A. Smith and John Fea have begun to speak of 'scholarship for the masses' and 'translation scholarship.' They view populist evangelicalism as 'a mission field' for evangelical scholars."[19]

THE FEARLESS CHRISTIAN UNIVERSITY AS A MISSION OUTPOST

Fearless Christian universities are not worried about mission drift or being seen as "going liberal." They know their mission well and communicate it effectively to all stakeholders.

We can return here to James Davison Hunter's idea of faithful presence mentioned in chapter 4: "A theology of faithful presence calls Christians to enact the shalom of God in the circumstances in which God has placed them and to actively seek it on behalf of others."[20] The fearless Christian university always looks for ways to pursue shalom using the resources it has at its disposal.

Possibility of Christianity in the Late Modern World (New York: Oxford University Press, 2010), 234.

19. Swartz, *Facing West*, 300.

20. Hunter, *To Change the World*, 278.

Administrators and trustees in such institutions are able to articulate this vision of faithful presence to those outside and to free up
faculty and staff members to proactively address contemporary issues.
The larger church truly needs the university to take these risks to be
ready for ministry in an unfolding future.

The fearless Christian university finds itself able to reach new populations of students in a time of declining enrollment by making a
priority of addressing their primary concerns. And the fearless education these students receive prepares them to be exactly the kinds of
future leaders institutions claim to want. Such leaders operate from a
position not of fear but of the love identified in Scripture.

HOPE, NOT FEAR

In the opening chapter, I wrote of Parker Palmer's treatment of the
biblical admonition "Be not afraid." He said that we have the opportunity to recognize fear but to act with courage anyway. This is the
defining motif of the fearless Christian university. It is concerned, to
adapt David Gushee's claim about Christian politics, with the common good more than its own identity: "A healthy Christian politics
concerns itself with the common good rather than the church's self-
interest narrowly conceived. This is an aspect of the modern Christian
social teaching tradition that becomes obvious upon the most limited
inspection. But it is also a matter in which the church has routinely
fallen short, because the church, and churches, are also human institutions susceptible to selfishness and narrow visions of the good."[21]

The hope-inspired focus of the Christian university is set squarely
on the transformation of its current and future students for the benefit of society. It is directly related to the mission of preparing future
leaders who combine academic, ethical, and spiritual maturity in an

21. David P. Gushee, *After Evangelicalism: The Path to a New Christianity*
(Louisville: Westminster John Knox Press, 2020), 148.

authentic whole. Arthur Holmes closed his book with a celebration of an imagined student, Pat:

> Pat is alert to the issues of the day: she feels the injustices of apartheid and admits there are ambiguities in Nicaragua. She listens to the other side, rather than reacting with an outburst of ridicule or anger. She measures her judgments before she acts, and before she votes. Her vote, in the end, is the kind of vote a democracy needs—informed, principled, and caring—not just blindly partisan. Her friends tell me she always gets to the heart of an issue. . . . Pat, I say, is an educated person.[22]

The fearless Christian university is built around students like Pat. All aspects of institutional life are designed to see her flourish for the benefit of a future we can only imagine. The final chapter offers a glimpse of what such an institution might look like.

22. Holmes, *Idea*, 104.

Envisioning the Fearless Christian University

I've argued throughout this book that the shifts required for an institution to become a fearless Christian university are clear and ready to hand for any university willing to face change boldly. The first essential shift, centering student experience, fits nicely with the mission statements most Christian universities have already. Second, moving beyond a transactional model of higher education to a transformational model requires faculty, administration, trustees, and stakeholders to be in frequent interaction. That is the only way to achieve the kind of alignment of values that fosters long-term change. Third, if institutions are to reach beyond traditional markets to a broader population of students whose concerns are notably different than those of past generations, they must move away from the fear-based culture-war posture that has defined far too much of Christian higher education. Today's students don't want to be a part of that. Fourth, and finally, coming to a deeper understanding of how the work of the Christian university differs from that of the church frees universities to be universities and to address the important issues of the day. Taken together, these important shifts can move Christian universities toward fearlessness.

What does a fearless Christian university look like? What are the levers that could initiate change in those institutions that have the courage to head down such a path? In this concluding chapter, I switch from analysis to projection, imagining life at two Christian institutions of higher education: Bartlet University[1] and Graham University.[2]

BARTLET UNIVERSITY AS A FEARLESS CHRISTIAN UNIVERSITY

A very excited group of students arrives on the campus of Bartlet University in the fall of 2025. Like the rest of Gen Z, they are a diverse bunch. While the plurality of students are white, the number of students of color—including Black, Hispanic, Asian, and mixed-race—make up nearly 40 percent of the incoming class. About one in four self-identify as gay or bisexual, yet they are fully aware of Bartlet's policy against premarital sex. They are predominantly female, echoing national trends among college students. While most have some religious background, there is much variability here as well. Some are from the sponsoring denomination. Others are generic evangelicals. Some are from mainline churches, where they served as leaders in their youth group. About a third have no prior faith commitments at all.

It would be a stretch to argue that all these students have come because of Bartlet's unique educational perspective. Some were recruited to an athletic team or music ensemble. Others have come because it was the right distance from home. Yet even these cannot fail to be exposed to Bartlet's core values and how they are expressed in university life. Every communication they have received as part of the

---

1. Yes, I'm a *West Wing* fan. But fans know that Jedediah Bartlet was Jesuit trained. As the Jesuits have historically done a great job of foregrounding academic life in the context of faith, it seemed appropriate. At the inauguration where I met Bill Robinson, mentioned in chapter 5, the keynote speaker was Avery Dulles, who articulated a very persuasive Jesuit educational philosophy.

2. Billy, not Franklin. Wheaton might stake a claim to the name, given the Billy Graham archives housed there. Montreat might also, as that's where the Grahams called home. Because Billy Graham attempted to present the gospel to the general population, it seemed fitting to lend his name to my example of a Christian university wanting to continue down that path.

admissions process has featured those values. Bartlet has a summer reading expectation that all incoming students read a book on successful Christian discourse. Because civic engagement is so central to Bartlet's mission, a common understanding of how the process works is essential.

The theme of engaging the world in positive ways is carried over into freshman orientation. Of course, there are the expected social bonding exercises and residence hall meetings. Yet a highlight of the program is a series of presentations on how a Christian university should address contemporary issues. Most important is the fact that these sessions are led by President Mark Ziegler, Dr. David Smith (professor of interpersonal communication), Dr. Susan Allen (associate professor of political science), and Rev. Andrea Jones (board chair and pastor of a nearby church of the sponsoring denomination).

These orientation sessions are not last-minute affairs. The four principals have been meeting at least once a month since the fall of 2024. The first of those meetings was a weekend retreat where they built relationships and discussed the complex issues they hoped to address the next fall.

Dr. Smith and Dr. Allen were not the only faculty members who had been exploring nuanced applications of Christian faith and theology to contemporary issues. The provost and the board's academic affairs committee had collaborated with the promotion and tenure committee to systematize how public scholarship would be counted alongside conference presentations, journal articles, and books. As a result, opinion pieces by Bartlet faculty and administrators regularly appeared in *Christianity Today*, the *Christian Century*, Religion News Service, and other venues. These, in turn, led to workshop invitations from local churches, seminaries, and Christian high schools.

In the first chapel of the academic year, chaplain Kate Harper and President Ziegler co-preach a sermon on the academic meaning of the biblical admonition "Be not afraid." Here is part of the message: "The heart of the educational enterprise [at Bartlet] is your unfolding story pursued simultaneously with the unfolding stories of all your classmates. The critical elements of institutional success are not based solely on high graduation rates and strong GRE scores, although these are important byproducts. The most important challenge of [Bartlet] must be to provide a place in which you can live out your story in ways that are sensitive to God's leading, academically grounded, faith affirming, and celebratory of your unique identity."[3]

This theme will be repeated throughout chapel services for the rest of the academic year.

Whenever the board of trustees is on campus, significant time is set aside for interaction with students and faculty. As much as possible, these interactions take place in small groups with the same participants at each meeting. This allows for the development of deeper relationships over time. The trustees, the faculty, and the students are all well aware of the need to keep trustees out of day-to-day administrative matters, but the relationships provide essential context for the policy discussions that are part of the board's purview.

The trustees regularly receive the above-mentioned public scholarship by Bartlet faculty and are encouraged to read them and engage with the authors. This engagement occurs not in a spirit of censoriousness but as a true example of civic dialogue.

Because institutional leadership has affirmed this public scholarship, there are no efforts to police what critics might claim is "woke ideology." The central topics of interest to students—economic inequality, human rights abuses, racial disparities, sexual orientation, political extremism—can be found in a variety of classes across the curriculum. Without discounting other disciplines, Bartlet leadership recognizes the importance of the liberal arts, humanities, and social sciences in appropriately interrogating these important issues.

Faculty at Bartlet are careful to acknowledge that there are a variety of perspectives on these topics and resist the temptation to offer theirs as the only one. When these differing perspectives come to light across disciplines, a teaching opportunity naturally arises. Special

---

3. This is a quote from my earlier book for incoming freshmen. John W. Hawthorne, *A First Step into a Much Larger World: The Christian University and Beyond* (Eugene, OR: Wipf and Stock, 2014), 11.

presentations, sometimes in chapel, provide a venue to demonstrate the critical thinking—but without demonizing opponents—that goes into analytic discourse.

When criticism comes from a feeder church, the sponsoring denomination's leaders, or evangelical media, the administration has a ready plan for response. President Ziegler foregrounds in every public speech he gives that Bartlet is *not* a church. Moreover, he argues that the university serves the church precisely by raising the questions the church is unable or unwilling to raise. He regularly cites the maxim "All truth is God's truth" as an acknowledgment that the work being done at Bartlet is the work God has called the community to do.

Such a stance makes Dr. Ziegler—as well as other Bartlet representatives—regularly sought out by secular media. Over time, these outlets will not simply look at the Liberty Universities of the world as an illustration of what Christian universities are like. Bartlet will achieve a reputation as a serious academic institution with deep Christian identity.

GRAHAM AS A UNIVERSITY READY FOR CHANGE

In the fall of 2025, Dr. Barbara Martin is beginning her third year as president of Graham University. A Graham alumna, she went on to earn a PhD in history and taught at another Christian university for twelve years before eventually becoming provost there and later accepting the call back to her alma mater. Since her undergraduate days, Graham has lived in the shadow of the very conservative Driscoll Christian University located an hour away.

She realized that the long-term success of Graham will not come from mirroring Driscoll. As she told the presidential search committee, a different stance is necessary. Having met Bartlet's Mark Zeigler at a Council of Independent Colleges conference, she arranged for her cabinet officers to travel to Bartlet to spend a couple of days.

Sensing that Graham's path forward will look more like Bartlet's than Driscoll's, she began to develop a plan for shifting the institutional culture toward fearlessness. She knows she needs to start with preparing her leadership team. She plans on inviting a small number of faculty members to the summer cabinet retreat to explore what such a change might mean.

The next step forward will involve the trustees. President Martin knows that she needs more trustees who understand the intricacies of the academic world (without sacrificing necessary financial expertise, relationship building, or gift-giving potential) and has already begun scouting potential board members. She invited Mark Ziegler to address the trustees at their fall meeting. In subsequent meetings over the year, she plans on inviting faculty and student leaders to the meetings for dialogue over what fearlessness would look like at Graham—not simply to mirror Bartlet but to find their own way.

She has encouraged the cabinet, local trustees, the faculty, and student leadership to read *The Idea of a Christian College* and to participate in a series of lunches to discuss what Holmes's argument means for Graham in the twenty-first century.[4] These lunches will result in a draft white paper outlining the fearless future of Graham University.

That draft document will then be shared with significant church and denominational leaders. They will be invited to provide input, but the primary reason for sharing is to indicate the kinds of conversations President Martin wants to encourage.

A work group representing the cabinet, key faculty members, and selected trustees will meet every other week to identify potential obstacles to the desired cultural change and potential solutions for those obstacles.[5] That work will be regularly reported in monthly faculty meetings both to keep the faculty engaged in the process and to elicit input for subsequent revisions.

The final step will be to examine Graham's marketing strategies. The admissions office is already investigating which currently absent mar-

---

4. Arthur Frank Holmes, *The Idea of a Christian College* (Grand Rapids: Eerdmans, 1975; 1987).

5. This idea is modeled on the Seattle Pacific example at the end of chapter 5.

kets might become available through a shift toward fearlessness. Strategies for reaching these new markets for fall 2026 and beyond are in process. Relatedly, a new approach to communicating with those markets and the broader public is required, especially given Gen Z shifts in social media usage. Examining what Bartlet has done will be helpful, but the unique features of a Graham education must be central.

As searches for faculty or administrative vacancies move forward for fall 2026, enthusiasm for the new direction is key. It is not necessary to remove occupants who are less enthusiastic, but clearly communicating that the change is occurring regardless is essential.

In short, this will be hard work for President Martin. There is no guarantee that it will be successful. Both insiders and external parties will throw sand in the gears. Nevertheless, it is critical work if Graham is to move out of Driscoll's shadow and establish a clear identity with a revitalized market.

How long will this process take? Institutional paradigm shifts can be achieved in five to seven years with the right leadership and a cooperative community. Yet the most important change, from fear to fearlessness, can begin paying dividends by as early as the end of the first year.

CONCLUSION

If Christian universities are to thrive in the coming decades, it will happen because they are forward thinking and not reactionary. Such a change in stance will alter the Christian university's relations with other segments of higher education, the broader culture, and the church.

Becoming a fearless Christian university will require courage from leaders, patience and trust from stakeholders, and renewed engagement from faculty and students. It is a risky endeavor for institutions comfortable with the status quo.

However, if even a handful of Christian universities find the courage to change their orientation, it could be transformational for Christian higher education. If this book prompts significant conversations to that end among administrators, trustees, faculty, staff, and students, then what I've been working toward for over four decades might be just beyond the horizon.

Acknowledgments

I'm grateful to Eerdmans for believing in this project, recognizing that an alternative approach to Christian higher education is necessary. Thanks especially to Lisa Ann Cockrel and James Ernest for their encouragement. I am deeply indebted to Laurel Draper, Jenny Hoffman, and especially Derek Keefe, whose patient editorial skills helped turn these words into a better version than what I could have imagined.

Over four decades, I've benefited from many conversation partners about the ideas in this book. I'm indebted to Steve Pusey, retired provost of Trevecca Nazarene University, Mike Roberts, retired sociologist from Eastern University and graduate school buddy, and Michael Wiese, now at Point Loma, as some of the earliest of these partners. At Warner Pacific, I'm glad to have known Cole Dawson, Art Kelly, Dennis Plies, Lou Foltz, and David Terrell and am grateful for our regular coffee conversations about life at the college. At Point Loma, Karl Martin, Jamie Gates, Dean Nelson, and Greg Crow stand out among many. At Spring Arbor, I am grateful for conversations with Mark Edwards, Mark Correll, Tom Holsinger-Friesen, and Jeremy Norwood. There have been a number of other conversation partners across Christian higher education, specifically Joshua Tom and Jennifer McKinney at Seattle Pacific, Kristin Kobes DuMez and Kevin Timpe at Calvin, Chris Gehrz at Bethel (MN), Jeff Tabone at Indiana Wesleyan, and Hannah Evans at the Springtide Research Institute.

Of course, I need to acknowledge the support of my family. Niki, Evgeni, Matt, and Yanling have been cheerleaders along the way. Grandchildren Rosa, Katya, Eric, and Anita have been a great diversion even if they aren't that aware of what I've been up to. My dogs Mazy and Juno have been faithful companions, letting me know it's time to stop writing and take them for a walk and with Juno sleeping under my desk while I write. Finally, I want to thank my wife, Jeralynne, who has walked beside me on this journey for nearly five decades.

Bibliography

Adams, Liam. "Christian Colleges Are Changing to Survive. Is It Working?" *Christianity Today*, September 9, 2020. https://tiny url.com/2ncum9pm.

Alberta, Tim. *The Kingdom, the Power, and the Glory: American Evangelicals in an Age of Extremism*. New York: HarperCollins, 2023.

Arnett, Jeffrey Jensen. *Emerging Adulthood: The Winding Road from the Late Teens through the Twenties*. 2nd ed. New York: Oxford University Press, 2015.

Association of Governing Boards of Universities and Colleges. "Board Member." Roles & Responsibilities. Accessed April 20, 2024. https://tinyurl.com/nxnpmt6r.

Balmer, Randall. *Bad Faith: Race and the Rise of the Religious Right*. Grand Rapids: Eerdmans, 2021.

———. "The Real Origins of the Religious Right." *Politico*, May 27, 2014. https://tinyurl.com/2d52p7jm.

Barna Group. "Five Causes Today's Teens Care About." *Barna Highlight*, March 13, 2023. https://tinyurl.com/34ya82sc.

Bean, Lydia. *The Politics of Evangelical Identity: Local Churches and Partisan Divides in the United States and Canada*. Princeton: Princeton University Press, 2014.

Bennett, Daniel. *Defending Faith: The Politics of the Christian Conservative Legal Movement*. Lawrence: University Press of Kansas, 2017.

Berger, Peter. *Invitation to Sociology: A Humanistic Perspective*. New York: Doubleday, 1963.

———. *The Sacred Canopy: Elements of a Sociological Theory of Religion*. Garden City, NY: Doubleday, 1967.

Bostock v. Clinton County, Georgia. 590 U.S. ___, 140 S. Ct. 1731 (2020). https://tinyurl.com/bdeeeydm.

Brenan, Megan. "Americans' Confidence in Higher Education Down Sharply." Gallup, July 11, 2023. https://tinyurl.com/5u8j4ty7.

Brueggemann, Walter. *The Prophetic Imagination*. 40th anniversary ed. Minneapolis: Fortress Press, 2018.

Bump, Philip. *The Aftermath: The Last Days of the Baby Boom and the Future of Power in America*. New York: Viking, 2023.

Bunch, Will. *After the Ivory Tower Falls: How College Broke the American Dream and Blew Up Our Politics—and How to Fix It*. New York: William Morrow, 2022.

Burge, Ryan. "How Many Evangelicals Are There?" Substack, December 28, 2023. https://tinyurl.com/yc8e7pze.

Chappell, Bill, and Vanessa Romo. "Tennessee House Votes to Expel 2 of 3 Democratic Members over Gun Protest." NPR, April 6, 2023. https://tinyurl.com/5n7ybe7b.

Coley, Jonathan S. *Gay on God's Campus: Mobilizing for LGBT Equality at Christian Colleges and Universities*. Chapel Hill: The University of North Carolina Press, 2018.

———. "Reframing, Reconciling, and Individualizing: How LGBTQ Activist Groups Shape Approaches to Religion and Sexuality." *Sociology of Religion* 81, no. 1 (Spring 2020): 45–67.

Colorado Christian University. "*Here We Stand* Is a Deeper Look at What Makes CCU 'Unapologetically Christian.'" 2022. https://www.ccu.edu/about/here-we-stand/.

Colson, Charles, and Nancy Pearcey. *How Now Shall We Live?* Carol Stream, IL: Tyndale House, 1999.

Cosper, Mike, host. *The Rise and Fall of Mars Hill*. Podcast. Christianity Today International, 2021–22. https://tinyurl.com/bdck6udp.

Council for Christian Colleges and Universities. "Membership Application." 2022. https://tinyurl.com/4pcs8ud7.

Crouch, Andy. *Culture Making: Recovering Our Creative Calling.* Downers Grove, IL: InterVarsity Press, 2008.

———. *Playing God: Redeeming the Gift of Power.* Downers Grove, IL: InterVarsity Press, 2013.

Dean, Kenda Creasy. *Almost Christian: What the Faith of Our Teenagers Is Telling the American Church.* New York: Oxford University Press, 2010.

Della Volpe, John. *Fight: How Gen Z Is Channeling Their Fear and Passion to Save America.* New York: St. Martin's Press, 2021.

Denton, Melinda Lundquist, and Richard Flory. *Back-Pocket God: Religion and Spirituality in the Lives of Emerging Adults.* New York: Oxford University Press, 2020.

Dockery, David S., and Gregory Alan Thornbury. *Shaping a Christian Worldview: The Foundations of Christian Higher Education.* Nashville: Broadman & Holman, 2002.

Downen, Robert, Lise Olsen, and John Tedesco. "Abuse of Faith." *Houston Chronicle,* February 10, 2019. https://tinyurl.com/y2fd6ffh.

Dreyfus, Hanna. "'The Liberty Way': How Liberty University Discourages and Dismisses Students' Reports of Sexual Assaults." *ProPublica,* October 14, 2021. https://tinyurl.com/yj2dw43w.

Drezner, Daniel W. "You Could Not Pay Me Enough to Be a College President." *Chronicle of Higher Education,* December 14, 2023. https://tinyurl.com/5y899d6c.

Du Mez, Kristin Kobes. *Jesus and John Wayne: How White Evangelicalism Corrupted a Faith and Fractured a Nation.* New York: Liveright Publishing, 2020.

Enns, Peter. *Curveball: When Your Faith Takes Turns You Never Saw Coming (or, How I Stumbled and Tripped My Way to Finding a Bigger God).* New York: HarperOne, 2023.

Evans, Rachel Held. *Evolving in Monkey Town: How a Girl Who Knew All the Answers Learned to Ask Questions.* Grand Rapids: Zondervan, 2010.

Favreau, Jon, Jon Lovett, Dan Pfieffer, and Tommy Vietor, hosts. "First Rule of Republican Fight Club." In *Pod Save America*. Podcast. Crooked Media, November 16, 2023. https://tinyurl.com/2kewkxva.

Fea, John. *Believe Me: The Evangelical Road to Donald Trump*. Grand Rapids: Eerdmans, 2018.

Fischman, Wendy, and Howard Gardner. *The Real World of College: What Higher Education Is and What It Can Be*. Cambridge, MA: The MIT Press, 2022.

FitzGerald, Frances. *The Evangelicals: The Struggle to Shape America*. New York: Simon and Schuster, 2017.

Flaherty, Colleen. "North Park Faculty Votes No Confidence in President." *Inside Higher Ed*, October 14, 2021. https://tinyurl.com/mrx3ks67.

————. "Too Small a Box? At Bryan College, Whose Name Honors a Famous Foe of Teaching Evolution, Faculty and Students Object to Being Required to Assert the Historicity of Adam and Eve." *Inside Higher Ed*, March 5, 2014. https://tinyurl.com/5d5p7wn5.

Fujimura, Makoto. *Culture Care: Reconnecting with Beauty for Our Common Life*. Downers Grove, IL: InterVarsity Press, 2017.

Gehrz, Chris. "It's Time to Drop the Faith Screen," *Pietist Schoolman*, January 24, 2023. https://tinyurl.com/32t7vc6w.

————, ed. *The Pietist Vision of Christian Higher Education: Forming Whole and Holy Persons*. Downers Grove, IL: IVP Academic, 2014.

Graham, Ruth. "What Really Caused an Evangelical College to Suspend a Professor?" *The Atlantic*, December 17, 2015. https://tinyurl.com/3tsjkn2d.

Green, Emma. "The Hidden Life of a Christian-College Professor." *The New Yorker*, June 30, 2022. https://tinyurl.com/4etwbjme.

Grove City College Board of Trustees. "Report and Recommendation of the Special Committee." Updated April 13, 2022. https://tinyurl.com/9xcu2nvx.

Gushee, David P. *After Evangelicalism: The Path to a New Christianity.* Louisville: Westminster John Knox Press, 2020.

Hammond, Michael D. "Christian Higher Education in the United States: The Crisis of Evangelical Identity." *Christian Higher Education* 18, no. 1–2 (2019): 3–15.

Hawthorne, John W. "Crisis in the Council for Christian Colleges and Universities: A Case Study of Fragmenting Evangelical Infrastructure." Paper presented at the Annual Meeting of the North Central Sociological Association, Chicago, IL, March 25, 2016.

———. *A First Step into a Much Larger World: The Christian University and Beyond.* Eugene, OR: Wipf and Stock, 2014.

Higher Learning Commission. "Criteria for Accreditation." 2022. https://tinyurl.com/2rkyj2fw.

Holmes, Arthur Frank. *The Idea of a Christian College.* Grand Rapids: Eerdmans, 1975; 1987.

Huiskes, Helen. "In the Fight over 'Wokeness,' Christian Colleges Feel Pressed to Pick a Side." *Chronicle of Higher Education,* August 31, 2023. https://tinyurl.com/ycyzkvuy.

Hunter, James Davison. *American Evangelicalism: Conservative Religion and the Quandary of Modernity.* New Brunswick, NJ: Rutgers University Press, 1983.

———. *Culture Wars: The Struggle to Define America.* New York: Basic Books, 1991.

———. *Evangelicals: The Coming Generation.* Chicago: University of Chicago Press, 1987.

———. *To Change the World: The Irony, Tragedy, and Possibility of Christianity in the Late Modern World.* New York: Oxford University Press, 2010.

Institute of Politics at Harvard Kennedy School. *Survey of Young Americans' Attitudes toward Politics and Public Service, 45th edition: March 13–22, 2023.* Updated April 24, 2023. https://tinyurl.com/mr33a2wf.

International Alliance for Christian Education. "Mission and Vision." https://iace.education/mission.

Jaschik, Scott. "Appeals Court Rejects Suit by College of the Ozarks." *Inside Higher Ed*, July 27, 2022. https://tinyurl.com/yptyjkpv.

———. "No-Confidence Vote at Cornerstone, Prior to Inauguration." *Inside Higher Ed*, October 24, 2021. https://tinyurl.com/2nzc bvd8.

Jenks, Andrew, producer. "Season 3: Jerry Falwell Jr. and Liberty University." In *Gangster Capitalism*. Podcast. Audacy Studios, 2021. https://tinyurl.com/2p9jj4ee.

Jones, Robert P. *The End of White Christian America*. New York: Simon and Schuster, 2015.

Kapic, Kelly M. "The Power of the Christian Quad." *Christianity Today* 63, no. 8 (Oct. 2019): 40–44.

Kelchen, Robert. "The Haves and Have-Nots of Higher Education." *Chronicle of Higher Education*, June 14, 2023. https://tinyurl.com/y4mu44yu.

Knox, Liam. "Grasping for a Foothold on the Enrollment Cliff." *Inside Higher Ed*, May 12, 2023. https://tinyurl.com/4u9w4pw9.

KY3. "Request Denied as College of the Ozarks Challenges Biden Administration over Gender Identity Directive." May 23, 2021. https://tinyurl.com/5yztpxr5.

Laats, Adam. *Fundamentalist U: Keeping the Faith in American Higher Education*. New York: Oxford University Press, 2018.

Lynch, Jamiel, and Andy Rose. "English Professor in Florida Says University Terminated His Contract after a Complaint over His Racial Justice Unit." CNN, March 16, 2023. https://tinyurl.com/2ybhda49.

Margolis, Michele F. *From Politics to the Pews*. Chicago: University of Chicago Press, 2018.

Mayfield, D. L. *Assimilate or Go Home: Notes from a Failed Missionary on Rediscovering Faith*. New York: HarperCollins, 2016.

———. "Deconversion: Part 1." *Healing is My Special Interest*. Substack, January 3, 2023. https://dlmayfield.substack.com/p/deconversion-part-1.

McKenna, David L. *Christ-Centered Higher Education: Memory, Mean-*

ing, and Momentum for the Twenty-First Century. Eugene, OR: Cascade Books, 2012.

Mennonite Church USA. "Forbearance in the Midst of Differences – 2015." July 2, 2015. https://tinyurl.com/yc85hnzy.

Merritt, Jonathan. *Jesus Is Better than You Imagined.* New York: Hachette Book Group, 2014.

National Center for Education Statistics. *Fast Facts: High School Graduation Rates.* Washington, DC: National Center for Education Statistics, 2023.

Palmer, Parker J. *The Courage to Teach.* 20th anniversary ed. San Francisco, CA: Jossey-Bass, 2017.

Parsons, Darlene. "The Justice Collective Documents Allegations That Cedarville University Violated the Higher Learning Commission Mandates." *The Wartburg Watch,* April 27, 2020. https://tinyurl.com/yv4dcuww.

Peterson, Amy. *Dangerous Territory: My Misguided Quest to Save the World.* Grand Rapids: Discovery House, 2017.

Pink Menno. "About." Accessed March 21, 2016. http://www.pinkmenno.org/history-vision/.

Post, Kathryn. "BYU Officially Restores Honor Code Ban on 'Same-Sex Romantic Behavior.'" Religion News Service, August 30, 2023. https://tinyurl.com/yck8dnem.

———. "Seattle Pacific University Targets LGBTQ Displays with New Policy, Say Critics." Religion News Service, September 29, 2023. https://tinyurl.com/y9fs8j2n.

———. "Wheaton College Restricts Employees' Ability to State Preferred Pronouns." Religion News Service, January 11, 2024. https://tinyurl.com/42unn59m.

Public Religion Research Institute. *The 2022 Census of American Religion.* February 24, 2023. https://tinyurl.com/y2x98bkh.

———. *Dueling Realities: Amid Multiple Crises, Trump and Biden Supporters See Different Priorities and Futures for the Nation.* October 19, 2020. https://tinyurl.com/mr47jt38.

———. *A Political and Cultural Glimpse into America's Future: Generation Z's Views on Generational Change and the Challenges*

and Opportunities Ahead. January 22, 2024. https://tinyurl.
com/268fx7xj.

———. *Threats to American Democracy Ahead of an Unprecedented Presidential Election.* October 25, 2023. https://tinyurl.com/
ywjt4jy2.

Robinson, William P. *Leading People from the Middle: The Universal Mission of Heart and Mind.* Provo, UT: Executive Excellence Publishing, 2002.

Rosenberg, Brian. *"Whatever It Is, I'm against It": Resistance to Change in Higher Education.* Cambridge, MA: Harvard Education Press, 2023.

"Save GCC from CRT." Updated November 10, 2021. https://tinyurl.
com/3xhcb96y.

"Save Grove City." 2022. https://savegrovecity.com/about.

Schaeffer, Francis. *How Should We Then Live? The Rise and Decline of Western Thought and Culture.* New York: Fleming Revell, 1976.

The School of the Ozarks, Inc., dba College of the Ozarks, Petitioner, v. Joseph R. Biden, Jr., President of the United States, et al. No. 21-2270 (8th Cir. 2022). https://tinyurl.com/52v2y8hp.

Schreiner, Laurie A. "What Good Is Christian Higher Education?" *Christian Higher Education* 17, no. 1–2 (2018): 33–49.

Seel, David John. *The New Copernicans.* Nashville: Thomas Nelson, 2018.

Silliman, Daniel. "Gordon College Settles with Professor It Said Was a Minister." *Christianity Today,* December 16, 2022. https://
tinyurl.com/25s9kfeu.

Silliman, Daniel, and Kate Shellnutt. "Wheaton College Releases Report on Its History of Racism." *Christianity Today,* September 14, 2023. https://tinyurl.com/frvwe755.

Smietana, Bob. "Taylor Professor Julie Moore Cited Jemar Tisby on Her Syllabus. Then She Lost Her Job." Religion News Service, May 3, 2023. https://tinyurl.com/4xwwdcxb.

Smietana, Bob, Morgan Lee, and Sarah Eekhoff Zylstra. "Two CCCU Colleges to Allow Same-Sex Married Faculty." *Christianity Today,* July 28, 2015. https://tinyurl.com/2vyssas3.

Smith, Christian. *American Evangelicalism: Embattled and Thriving.* Chicago: University of Chicago Press, 1998.

Smith, Christian, Kari Marie Christoffersen, Hilary Davidson, and Patricia Snell Herzog. *Lost in Transition: The Dark Side of Emerging Adulthood.* New York: Oxford University Press, 2011.

Springtide Research Institute. *The State of Religion & Young People 2023: Exploring the Sacred.* Winona, MN: Springtide Research Institute, 2023.

SPU Faculty Action. "SPU LGBTQIA+ Timeline." Accessed April 20, 2024. https://tinyurl.com/yc3xkw2w.

Statista. "Resident Population of the United States by Sex and Age as of July 1, 2022." Updated October 2, 2023. https://tinyurl.com/j3a529t7.

Stearns, Richard. *The Hole in Our Gospel: The Answer That Changed My Life and Might Just Change the World.* Nashville: Thomas Nelson, 2009.

Swartz, David R. *Facing West: American Evangelicals in an Age of World Christianity.* New York: Oxford University Press, 2020.

Takahama, Ellen. "Seattle Pacific University Faculty Votes 'No Confidence' in Leadership after Board Upholds Discriminatory Hiring Policy." *The Seattle Times,* April 21, 2021. https://tinyurl.com/49dxbjn7/.

Taylor, Barbara Brown. *Holy Envy: Finding God in the Faith of Others.* New York: HarperOne, 2019.

Tisby, Jemar. *The Color of Compromise: The Truth about the American Church's Complicity in Racism.* Grand Rapids: Zondervan, 2019.

———. "An Open Letter to the Board of Trustees at Grove City College." Substack, May 18, 2022. https://tinyurl.com/u8n82cte.

US Bureau of Labor Statistics. "College Enrollment and Work Activity of Recent High School and College Graduates Summary." Last modified April 26, 2023. https://tinyurl.com/3unhhwn9.

Whitford, Emma. "Enrollment Marches Downward." *Inside Higher Ed,* January 12, 2022. https://tinyurl.com/mpkpns2c.

Wingfield, Mark. "Hardin-Simmons Faculty Overwhelmingly Vote

No Confidence in President." Baptist News Global, October 27, 2022. https://tinyurl.com/48c27bmh.

Worthen, Molly. *Apostles of Reason: The Crisis of Authority in American Evangelicalism.* New York: Oxford University Press, 2014.

Yancey, Philip. *Where the Light Fell.* New York: Convergent Publishing, 2021.

YouGov. "CBS News Poll – September 5–8, 2023." Updated September 8, 2023. https://tinyurl.com/3zx38tke.

Zahneis, Megan. "They Put Their Pronouns in Their Email Signatures. Then the University Dismissed Them." *Chronicle of Higher Education,* April 26, 2023. https://tinyurl.com/yc6md92z.

Zierman, Addie. *When We Were on Fire: A Memoir of Consuming Faith, Tangled Love, and Starting Over.* New York: Convergent Books, 2013.

Index

and, 3–4, 78, 109; homeschooled,
23n10, 38; mission relevance for,
23; nontraditional, 4–5, 91–92;
plausibility structures of, 37–40,
117; religious commitments of,
5–6, 9, 89, 92–93; social issues
and, 6–7, 13, 50, 53–54, 55, 100,
113–14; traditional, 5, 86, 91–92;
trustees and, 50, 106–12, 127
Swartz, David, 123, 124

Taylor, Barbara Brown, 40–41
Tisby, Jemar, 12
To Change the World (Hunter), 123
transactional learning, 25–26, 28, 86
transformational learning, 28–29,
125–26, 127

trustees: administrators and, 13,
69, 70, 72, 81; faculty and, 68–73,
78, 80–81; role of, 76, 77, 80–81,
125; stakeholder pressures on, 13,
70; students and, 50, 106–12, 127;
worlds of, 76–77, 80, 81

Union University, 53

Viguerie, Richard, 48

Weyrich, Paul, 47–48
Whitworth University, 54
World Vision, 123
Worthen, Molly, 2, 30

zombie institutions, 121–22
Zoomers, 9, 39, 89, 95–102, 104–7